Cooperative Learning Structures
for
Classbuilding

Miguel Kagan, Laurie Robertson, and Spencer Kagan

COOPERATIVE LEARNING

COOPERATIVE LEARNING

Kagan Cooperative Learning
1160 Calle Cordillera
San Clemente, CA 92673

1 (800) WEE CO-OP

ISBN: 1-879097-29-X

Table of Contents

Structures-at-a-Glance

Corners

1. Teacher Announces Corners
2. Students Think & Write
3. Students Go to Corners
4. Pairs Discuss

Find-Someone-Who

1. Students Mix & Pair
2. Student Questions Partner
3. Partner Checks
4. Reverse Roles

Formations

1. Teacher Announces Formation
2. Students Create Formation

Kagan, Robertson & Kagan: *Cooperative Learning Structures for Classbuilding*©

Kagan Cooperative Learning • 1(800) WEE CO-OP

Guess-the-Fib

1. Students Write Three Statements
2. One Student Reads Statements
3. Teammates Discuss Statements
4. Teammates Guess

Inside/Outside Circle

1. Students Form Circles
2. Student Shares with Partner
3. Reverse Roles
4. Students Rotate

Line-Ups

1. Teacher Describes the Line
2. Students Line Up
3. Pairs Discuss

Structures-at-a-Glance

Mix-Freeze-Group

1. Students "Mix"
2. Students "Freeze"
3. Students "Group"

Mix-N-Match

1. Students "Mix"
2, Students "Freeze"
3. Students "Match"

Similarity Groups

1. Teacher Announces Topic
2. Students Form Groups
3. Paris Discuss

Kagan, Robertson & Kagan: *Cooperative Learning Structures for Classbuilding*©
Kagan Cooperative Learning • 1(800) WEE CO-OP

Stir-the-Class

1. **Students Stand in Groups**
2. **Students Huddle**
3. **Students Rotate**
4. **Huddle Again & Praise**

Who-am-I

1. **Cards Placed on Backs**
2. **Students Mix & Pair**
3. **Student Questions Partner**
4. **Reverse Roles**
5. **Students Become Helpers**

Preface

This book is dedicated to you — a teacher dedicated to building the cooperative classroom: A classroom in which each student explores the content and is an active member of a learning community; a classroom in which each student celebrates the diversity of every other classmate; a classroom that each student is excited to enter every day and is sad to leave at the end of the year; a classroom that prepares students to become better people who will make the world a better place.

What is Classbuilding?

This book is about Classbuilding. "Well, what in the world is Classbuilding?" you ask. As you would rightfully respond to your students: "If you want to truly understand something, you'll have to investigate it yourself." So look it up!

What's that? Couldn't find Classbuilding in the dictionary? Well it should be in the dictionary as well as every pedagogical manual, but you're right, it's not. So here's a crack at a definition:

> **Classbuilding** (klas·bild·ing), *c*1980. *v.* The process by which a room full of individuals with different backgrounds and experiences become a caring community of active learners.

Pretty simple right? Right. There a few interesting things to note about that little concocted definition. First of all, notice the date. Classbuilding is dated circa 1980. The move to create a more cooperative and democratic classroom in which there is a high premium on student autonomy and interaction is by no means a new movement. The date refers to the term itself. The name classbuilding was coined around this time by Spencer Kagan who thought that the term used to that point, "Whole class inclusion activities," was too much of a mouthful!

The second, and perhaps most noteworthy part of the concocted definition is that classbuilding is a verb; it is an action word; it is a process. Classbuilding doesn't happen. Classbuilding is done!

And finally, one addendum: The term Classbuilding should be used quite loosely. Classbuilding refers to any classroom practices that involve the whole classroom which result in improved classroom climate.

Why do Classbuilding?

"So tell me, why do I want to do classbuilding in my class?" OK. You asked so here it goes. The rationale for doing classbuilding is manyfold. Classbuilding is great for getting students acquainted with one another at the beginning of the year. Classbuilding throughout the year promotes the liking and respecting of teammates and classmates. Students interact with one another in an open, nonthreatening environment creating mutual support and promoting self-esteem. Students are active, and the classroom becomes fun and energizing. Students enjoy the class and the school more. The classroom runs smoothly and less time is spent on management and more time on active learning. Students learn lifelong interpersonal skills and are better prepared to function in an increasingly pluralistic society. And the world is a little nicer place because of it. Good enough?

By now you're probably saying to yourself, "Yeah, yeah, that's all fine and dandy, I already know all this. That's why I became a teacher and that is why I picked up this book. If you want to give me anything, don't give me a lecture. GIVE ME ACTIVITIES THAT I CAN USE IN MY CLASSROOM! TODAY!"

OK. OK. Got the message. We'll get to that in a minute. Just one more thing. There are many ways to create a positive classroom climate, and therefore many different ways to do classbuilding. This book describes one method of doing classbuilding. Let's take a quick peek at a few other methods.

Types of Classbuilding

The most broad-based classbuilding technique is through classroom restructuring. Cooperatively structured classrooms contribute greatly to a positive class tone. Students work together cooperatively in teams, help others when help is requested and request help when help is needed. Frequent class meetings are

Kagan, Robertson & Kagan: *Cooperative Learning Structures for Classbuilding*©
Kagan Cooperative Learning • 1 (800) WEE CO-OP

set up for mutual support, to address issues and to improve class functioning. Class goals are established in which all students are positively interdependent in their striving toward the class goal, giving students a common mission and a sense of classroom identity. Also, empowering students by allowing each to participate in the decision-making process gives students a sense of classroom belonging and ownership. How students interact with one another, how students feel about class and school is largely a function of how we structure our classrooms and the behavioral expectations we set forth. A list of resources on structuring the classroom cooperatively is provided in the **Cooperative Learning** section of the resource list at the back of this book.

Another form of classbuilding is through explicit classroom instruction of prosocial behaviors. Providing students with prosocial skills such as caring, cooperating, giving, sharing, empathy, tolerance, peacemaking and conflict resolution skills is another route to building the caring classroom. There are a variety of great literature selections as well as other resources available for teaching social skills. A list of resources for teaching prosocial skills is provided in the **Social Skills** section of the resource list at the back of this book.

Classbuilding may also be done by validating the backgrounds and experiences of individuals and cultural groups. Self-Esteem activities are designed to affirm individuals' competence and individuality. Students learn to value their own uniqueness and respect themselves; they are therefore more prepared to extend that respect to others. Multicultural activities celebrate the richness and diversity of different cultures. These classbuilding techniques strive to create an inclusive classroom in which all students feel that they are important members. See the **Inclusive Classroom** section of the resource list.

And finally there are classbuilding activities. These are fun, usually energizing activities which involve networking opportunities for all students of the classroom. And that is what this book is all about. Sound good? It is. Want to get the most out of this book? Read on.

How to Get the Most Out of This Book

We selected our eleven favorite cooperative learning structures for classbuilding. Each structure is energizing and provides opportunities for students to work (or play) with classmates. The

book is arranged alphabetically by structure. For each structure, we have provided a description, the step-by-step procedures, some hints, the inherent benefits of the structure, the basic principles, variations on the structure, and tons of content ideas. Following each structure there are blackline masters for different activities to do with the structures. Think of these as sample activities. We have provided activities in a variety of content areas for a variety of grade levels. There are a number of really great classbuilding activities here. These, however, are only samples.

A structure is a content-free way to organize student interaction. It is the step-by-step of how students interact with each other. When you add some content to the structure, *VOILÁ*, an activity is born. With new content, you get a brand new activity every time. So really, the structures are like an activity factory. Just put the content in one end and an activity pops out the other. A structure can be used over and over and over and over... well, we think you get the picture.

To get the most out of this book, don't just do the activities, master the structures. Read them; try them; make them your own. With these eleven structures, and a little imagination, you can create an endless array of classbuilding activities!

We hope you enjoy these structures as much as we enjoy providing them!

Laurie Robertson

Corners

As students move to corners of the room, they discover there are a variety of points of view on an issue—and that theirs' is but one of many valid ways of thinking.

In Corners, the teacher announces a topic and gives students a choice of four alternatives. Any preference can be the focus, such as favorite season, intended profession, or even which of four types of shoes a student would chose to be. Students go to the corner of the room representing their choice. For example, all the tennis shoe people go to one corner, the hiking boot people go to another. Students then share reasons for their choice with a partner in their corner.

Corners is designed to allow students to know and accept themselves and others more. Corners is particularly good for promoting an appreciation of individual differences. Students realize they can be accepted while making choices which are different from their classmates.

❶ Teacher Announces Corners

Announce the alternatives for each corner of the room. "Think about circus performers. If you were to take a job in the circus, which of these four would you choose: An Acrobat, The Master of Ceremonies, The Lion Tamer, or The Clown."

❷ Students Think & Write

Give students a bit of silent think time to make their choice. Have them write the name or their choice on a slip of paper. "Without discussing with other students, write the name of your corner on a slip of paper."

4 Pairs Discuss

Have pairs in each corner discuss the reasons for their preferences. "In pairs, discuss why you chose the corner you did."

3 Students Go to Corners

Tell students to go to their selected corners. "Walk to your corner of the room and find a partner to talk with, someone not on your team."

Hints

★ **Number Corners.** Before going to the corners, have students write down the number of their choice without discussing their choice with anyone else. This avoids students grouping by friendship rather than opinion.
★ **Use Visuals.** Post a title, and/or visual in each corner of the classroom, especially for younger students.
★ **Equal Alternatives.** Select alternatives that will be roughly equally divided.
★ **No Loners.** If by chance only one student chooses a corner, validate the choice but then ask the student to choose his/her second favorite choice to have someone to discuss with.
★ **Equal Time.** Give students equal time to share in pairs, saying something like "Ones, you have one minute to share... Twos, it is your turn to share."

Benefits

• Students value and appreciate individual differences. • Students create links and bonds with classmates, getting to know them better. • Classmates who choose the same corner feel mutual support. • Students hear multiple perspectives and a range of reasoning processes. • Students relate content to personal preferences. • Students become comfortable expressing and explaining personal preferences.

Ideas for My Class!

Classbuilding

My favorite...
- **Pie:** Apple, Pumpkin, Cherry, Lemon Meringue
- **Type of food:** Mexican, Italian, Chinese, American
- **Sport:** Baseball, Basketball, Soccer, Football
- **Fast food:** Carl's Jr., Burger King, Wendy's, Taco Bell
- **Car:** Porsche, Cadillac, Pick-up, Limousine
- **Hobby:** Bicycling, Roller Skating, Skateboarding, Skiing
- **Season:** Spring, Summer, Winter, Fall
- **Vegetable:** Spinach, Zucchini, Cauliflower, Broccoli
- **Fruit:** Apple, Orange, Banana, Peach
- **Art type:** Charcoal, Paint, Clay, Pen
- **Instrument:** Wind, String, Percussion, Brass
- **Recess activity:** Jump rope, Swings, Bars, Ball game

I would rather be...
- **Career:** Athlete, Entertainer, Politician, Doctor
- **Band member:** Guitarist, Drummer, Pianist, Vocalist
- **Circus:** Lion Tamer, Acrobat, Clown, Emcee
- **Boat:** Row boat, Speed boat, Sail boat, Cruise ship

I am/ I have...
- **Birth order:** Only Child, Youngest, Middle, Oldest
- **Siblings:** None, One, Two, Three or more

Mathematics

My favorite...
- **Math process:** Addition, Subtraction, Multiplication, Division
- **Number:** One, Seven, Ten, Five
- **Shape:** Square, Circle, Rectangle, Triangle

I would rather be...
- **Career:** Computer Programmer, Teacher, Accountant, Engineer
- **Shape:** Square, Circle, Rectangle, Triangle

I am/ I have...
- **Type of graph:** Pie chart, Bar graph, Line graph, Picture graph
- **Answer to a problem:** 1/2, 1/4, 1/3, 1/5
- **Placement:** Ones, Tens, Hundreds, Thousands

Variations

Sides Instead of having four alternatives, have only two sides. Use Sides when you want students to take sides to an issue. It provides the basis for constructive controversy. Alternatively, three or five choices may be used instead of the usual four corners.

Corners Teams Form discussion groups consisting of one student from each corner. The discussion is enriched by multiple perspectives since each student has a different viewpoint or background.

Response Modes

- *Rallyrobin in Corners* Individuals in corners pair up to Rallyrobin reasons for their choice. Student 1 gives one reason; then Student 2 gives a reason; then Student 1 gives another.

- *Roundrobin in Corners* While in corners, student form groups of four and Roundrobin the reasons for their choices.

- *Three-Step in Corners* Once students are in Corners, do a Three-Step Interview.

- *Square in Corners* Sometimes have students in corners discuss in teams rather than in pairs.

- *Paraphrase in Corners* After having some students from a corner share with the class their reasons for choosing their corner, have all students form pairs in their corners to paraphrase the ideas from other corners. In this way, students become active listeners to points of view different from their own.

Principles

Positive Interdependence Students' explanations or their reasons for choosing a corner enriches the thinking of other students.

Individual Accountability Students are held accountable for their choice by having them write down their selection. Students are held accountable for explaining their choice to a partner.

Equal Participation Students are given equal opportunity to share.

Simultaneous Interaction Half the class is speaking at once as students discuss in pairs.

Science

My favorite...
- **Farm animal:** Horse, Sheep, Goat, Cow
- **Pet:** Dog, Cat, Fish, Rabbit
- **Sea life:** Shark, Dolphin, Octopus, Whale
- **Bird:** Parrot, Dove, Eagle, Blue Jay
- **Tree:** Oak, Willow, Pine, Sycamore
- **Flower:** Daisy, Rose, Lily, Tulip

I would rather be...
- **Profession:** Astronomer, Chemist, Physicist, Biologist
- **Dinosaur:** Triceratops, Pterodactyl, T-Rex, Brontosaurus
- **Wild animal:** Lion, Zebra, Giraffe, Elephant
- **On planet:** Mars, Jupiter, Saturn, Pluto

I am/ I have...
- **Matter:** Solid, Liquid, Gas
- **Water cycle:** Raindrop, Lake, River, Ocean
- **Organ:** Heart, Kidney, Brain, Stomach
- **Simple machine:** Lever, Gear, Wheel, Pulley
- **Body system:** Skeletal, Digestive, Muscular, Circulatory

Social Studies

My favorite...
- **Holiday:** Christmas, Halloween, Easter, Thanksgiving
- **Social science:** Psychology, Sociology, History, Anthropology

I would rather be...
- **Time period:** Colonial, Wild West, Roaring 20's, 2010
- **Historical character:** Ghandi, Washington, Lincoln, Churchill
- **Career:** Politician, Doctor, Lawyer, Teacher
- **Indian tribe:** Sioux, Cherokee, Apache, Comanchee
- **Visit:** Africa, Europe, Asia, Australia
- **Famous person:** Musician, Actor, Athlete, Artist

Language Arts

My favorite...
- **Story character:** Cinderella, Peter Pan, Jack, Goldilocks
- **Type of book:** Mystery, Adventure, Fantasy, Science Fiction
- **Type of writing:** Imaginative, Informative, Opinionated, Reporting
- **Metaphor:** Flowing River, Babbling Brook, Calm Lake, Rough Seas
- Book we read
- **Author:** Steinbeck, Hemingway, Twain, Poe
- **Poet:** Frost, Shakespeare, Cummings, Sandberg
- Poem we read
- Four endings to a story
- Story we read
- Vocabulary words

I am/ I have...
- **Sentence:** Question, Statement, Exclamation, Command
- **Part of speech:** Noun, Verb, Adjective, Adverb
- **Grammatical error:** Run-on, Fragment, Misspelling, Punctuation
- **Punctuation:** Period, Question mark, Exclamation mark, Semi-colon
- **Literary term:** Metaphor, Simile, Personification, Hyperbole

Corners

My favorite holiday is...
Christmas

My favorite holiday is...
Halloween

My favorite holiday is...
Easter

My favorite holiday is...

Fourth of July

When I grow up, I want to be...

Doctor

Firefighter

Actor/Actress

Police Officer

When I grow up, I want to be...

Writer

Politician

Nurse

Salesperson

If I lived in the ocean...

Whale

Seal

Shark

Dolphin

If I worked in the circus...

Acrobat

Lion Tamer

Emcee

Clown

My favorite season is...

Winter

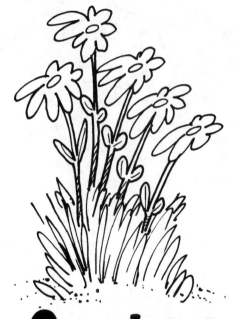

Spring

Summer

Fall

I am most like a...

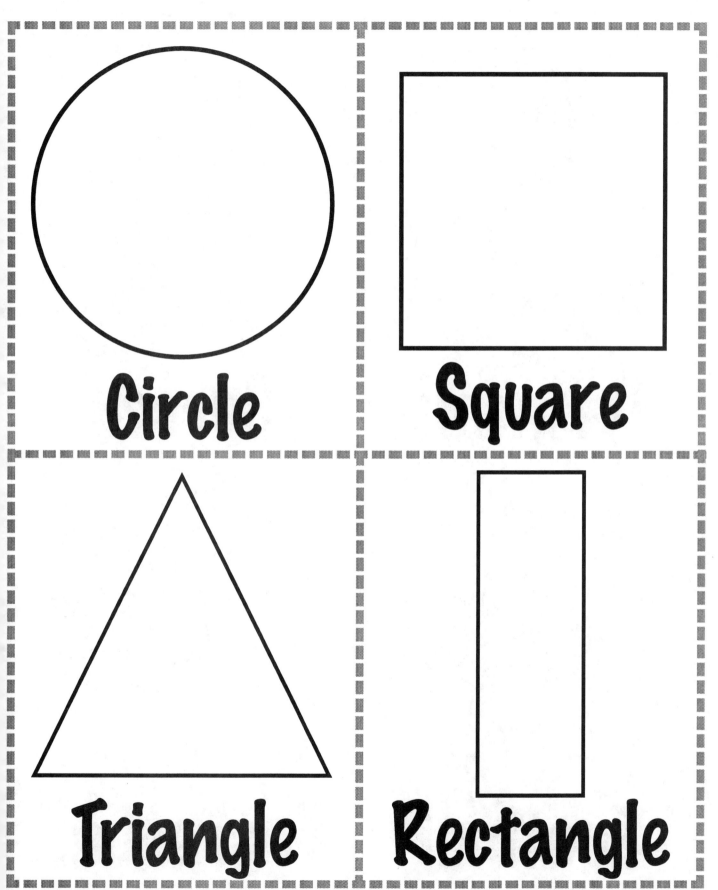

Circle

Square

Triangle

Rectangle

I prefer to play...

Baseball

Soccer

Football

Basketball

I would rather be...

Bicycling

Skiing

Swimming

Dancing

I would prefer to be a...

Drummer

Singer

Guitarist

Pianist

I would rather live in the...

Wild West

Space Age

Stone Age

Medieval Times

My favorite fairy tale is..

Little Red Riding Hood

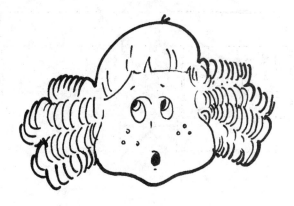

Goldilocks

Cinderella

Snow White

I prefer to go to the...

Mall

Museum

Park

Movies

Find-Someone-Who

Students are excited, circulating through the classroom, forming and reforming pairs, writing answers on a worksheet which their partner signs. Students try to "Find Someone Who" knows an answer; they then become "Someone Who Knows."

Students each receive a worksheet. The worksheet has questions like, "Find someone who knows the name of this flower." Students mingle in the classroom until they find a partner. Partners then ask each other questions from the worksheet. If a partner knows an answer, he/she shares and the other student writes it on the worksheet in his/her own words. Partners sign under the answer after checking to make sure that it was correctly written. Students can receive only one answer from a partner and then circulate to find another partner. When students finish their worksheet, they become helpers by sitting down and becoming a resource for others who can ask them any question.

One very nice feature of this structure is that students who initially knew none of the answers, after filling in one or two answers, become a resource for others because the have become "someone who knows."

❶ Students Mix & Pair

With worksheets in hand, students circulate through the room until they find a partner. "I want you to mix around the room until you find a partner. When you find a partner, you can ask each other questions until you find a partner who knows. If your partner knows an answer, fill in the box in your own words on the Find Someone Who form, and then have your partner sign your form to show he or she agrees."

❷ Student Questions Partner

One student asks his/her partner one question on the worksheet. The partner shares the answer if he or she knows it. Then the student writes the answer in his/her own words.

4 Reverse Roles

Students switch roles. The student who asked the first question tries to answer his or her partner's question.

Finish the Form: Students mix and pair again, with a new partner each time until they finish the Find-Someone-Who form.

3 Partner Checks

The partner checks to see that the answer is written correctly. If the partner agrees with the written answer, he or she signs the form on the line under the answer.

Hints

★ **Hand Signals.** Have students raise one hand as they walk until they find a partner. This makes it easy to spot those still looking for a partner.
★ **Students Provide Content.** Prior to playing People Hunt and Fact Bingo, have students turn in one little known characteristic that they would like everyone to know to use for the form.
★ **One Answer Each.** Remind students they can get only one answer from a partner and then must circulate to find another partner.

Benefits

• All classmates help each other reach the class goal. • Even students who initially knew no answers become a valuable source for others. • Students are actively involved; the class has the tone of an exciting treasure hunt. • Knowledgeable students are valued by peers.

Ideas for My Class!

Classbuilding

Find Someone Who...
- Has brown hair
- Has a dog and a cat
- Likes to eat pizza
- Is the same height
- Is wearing pink
- Was born in the summer
- Isn't wearing socks
- Has 4 pockets today
- Has a sister
- Favorite color is blue
- Has a striped shirt on
- Wears glasses
- Has a shirt with three buttons
- Rides a bike to school
- Can sing the ABC's
- Is wearing a digital watch
- Can answer a riddle
- Skis in the winter

Mathematics

Find Someone Who...
- Can solve 2+2
- Can count by twos to 40
- Can repeat the pattern (Triangle, Square, S, T, S, _ _ _ _)
- Can name geometric shapes
- Can measure
- Can add numbers with decimals
- Can divide multi-digit numbers
- Can write out numbers
- Can identify a computer part
- Can extend a number pattern
- Can locate a point on grid
- Can name the money value
- Can convert a decimal to percent
- Can demonstrate the preservation of equality

Variations

3 Questions Allow students to ask a partner up to three questions, trying to find a question the partner knows.

People Hunt Students are given a People Hunt form. The form has a list of characteristics, one corresponding to each student in the class. Students "hunt" for the student that fits the characteristic listed on the People Hunt form. Students pair up and ask each other one question. "Are you the person who has bungee jumped?" When students find the person matching the listed characteristic, that student signs the form. The class continues until all students finish their People Hunt forms. People Hunt may also be played in which students get a form with questions for themselves. Then, students "hunt" for someone who is like them based on those characteristics.

Info Search Start with a topic on which all students have no information. Every student gets an Info Search form which is a worksheet with questions on it. If there are ten questions on the worksheet, ten students get an answer sheet with one answer filled in. Students then play the game just like Find-Someone-Who. Soon all students have all the answers.

Find-Those-Who This variation is played just like Find-Someone-Who except students circulate about the classroom in pairs or teams searching for another pair or team that has the answers.

Fact Bingo A bingo type card is made up. The cells each have a fact about a student. Students circulate and try to fill the card or get bingo by locating classmates who fit the description. Classmates sign the cell when they are correctly identified.

Principles

Positive Interdependence Students need information from their partner; they cannot do the task alone.

Individual Accountability Students are accountable for active listening and writing. Partners check to make sure they have written what was said before signing off on it.

Equal Participation Students take turns asking and answering questions.

Simultaneous Interaction Half the class is speaking at once as students are questioning in pairs.

Science

Find Someone Who...

- Can identify a dinosaur
- Can identify a simple machine
- Knows a part of the solar system
- Can label a part of a plant
- Can identify a cloud type
- Knows a part of the water cycle
- Knows the symbol for the chemical element
- Can explain the science vocabulary word
- Can identify the rock or mineral
- Can name the bone or muscle
- Can identify the weather condition
- Can identify the body part
- Knows the organ function

Social Studies

Find Someone Who...

- Knows the Pledge of Allegiance
- Can identify a land form
- Knows the capital
- Can identify the time zone
- Can identify the Indian tribe
- Can identify the famous explorer
- Can identify the Amendment
- Can recognize the constitutional right
- Can name one of the 13 colonies
- Can explain supply and demand
- Define a geographical term
- Can identify the continent or ocean
- Can locate the coordinates
- Can distinguish between needs and wants
- Can explain the difference in political parties
- Can name which branch of government
- Can name which level of government

Language Arts

Find Someone Who...

- Can identify the part of a book
- Knows the the vowel sound
- Knows if it is fact or fiction
- Can identify the part of a friendly letter
- Knows the correct spelling
- Can distinguish fiction from non-Fiction
- Can identify the cause and effect
- Can identify main idea
- Can differentiate fact and opinion
- Can alphabetize a set of words

- Knows the abbreviation
- Can write an adjective for the noun listed
- Can correctly place quotation marks
- Knows the word definition and part of speech
- Can distinguish suffix from prefix
- Knows a rhyming word for the listed word
- Can make the consonant sound
- Can summarize the plot
- Has read the book

Find-Someone-Who

Kagan, Robertson & Kagan: *Cooperative Learning Structures for Classbuilding*©
Kagan Cooperative Learning • 1(800) WEE CO-OP

Find Someone Who...
can name this shape.

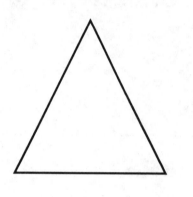

_____

_____

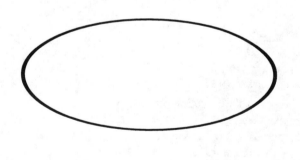

_____

_____

My name _____
_____

Find Someone Who...

My name

Find Someone Who...

name

Find Someone Who...

Can sing their ABC's

Can name this animal

Can tie their shoe

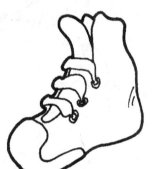

Can name five colors

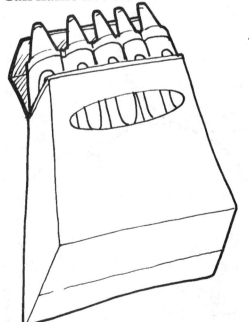

Can count to 20.

My name _____

Find Someone Who...
can name a farmyard animal.

Name _____

Animal _____

Name _____

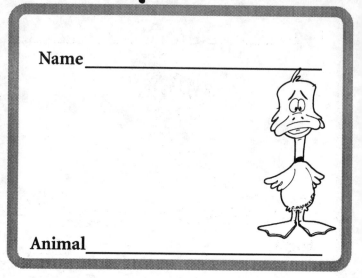

Animal _____

Name _____

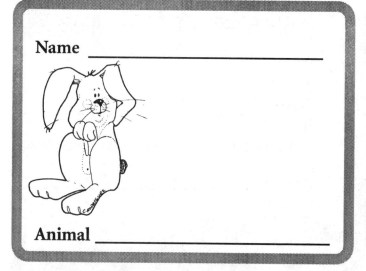

Animal _____

Name _____

Animal _____

Name _____

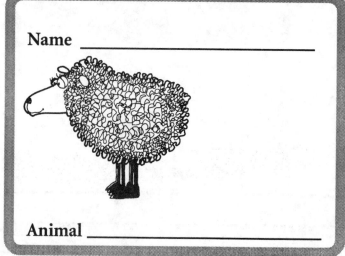

Animal _____

Name _____

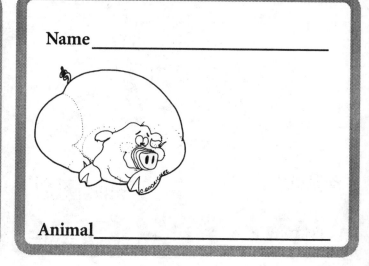

Animal _____

Find Someone Who...
can name the geographical formation

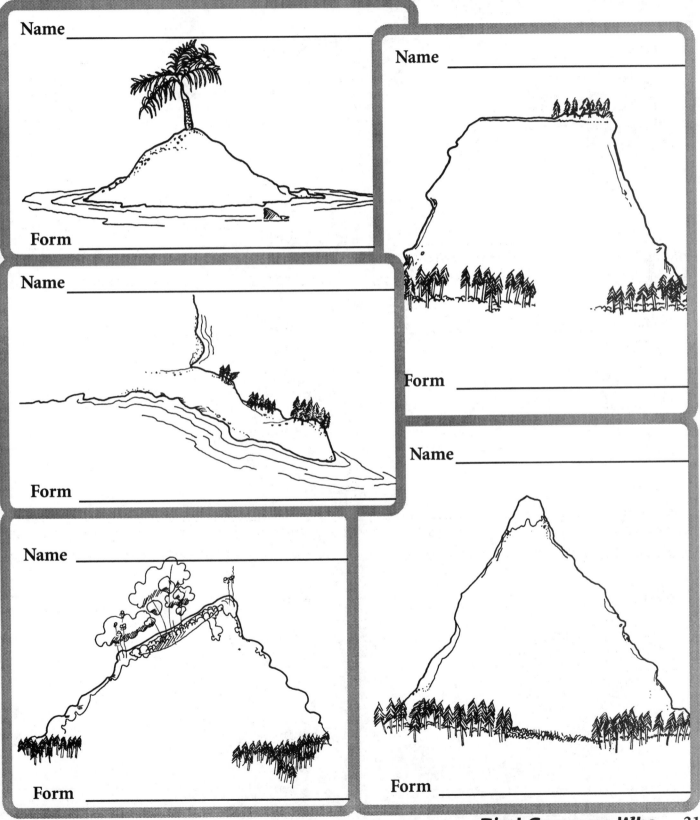

Name _____

Form _____

Name _____

Form _____

Name _____

Form _____

Name _____

Form _____

Name _____

Form _____

Find Someone Who...
can name the dinosaur.

Dinosaur_____

Name _____

Dinosaur_____

Name _____

Dinosaur_____

Name _____

Dinosaur_____

Name _____

Dinosaur_____

Name _____

Find Someone Who...

Name _____	Name _____
_____	_____

Name _____	Name _____
_____	_____

Name _____	Name _____
_____	_____

Find Someone Who...
knows how much is shaded.

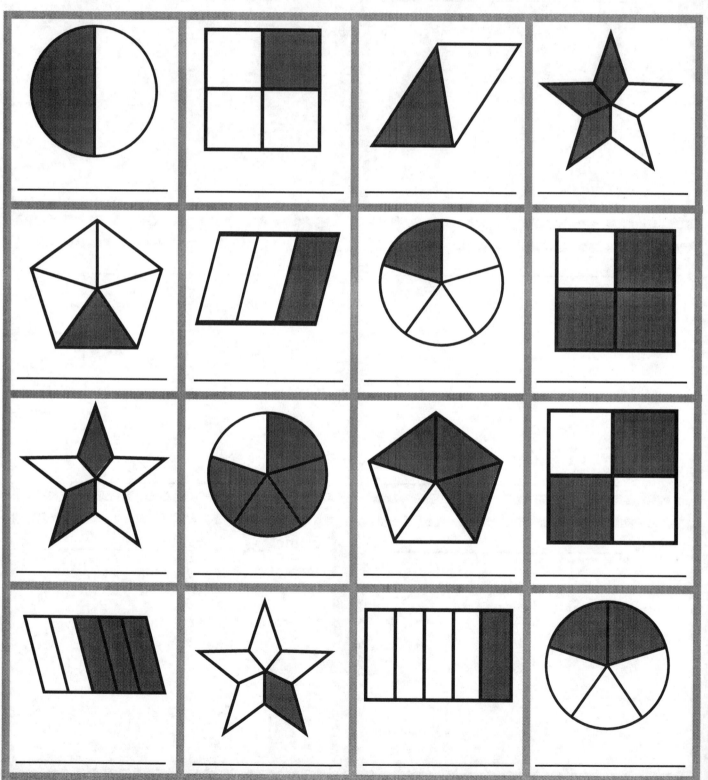

Find Someone Who...

Find Someone Who...

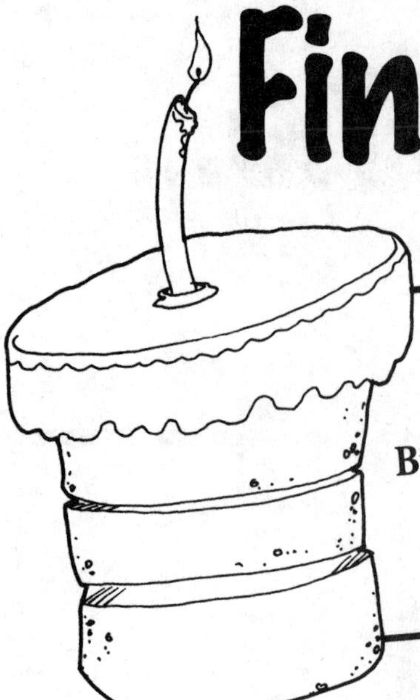

Is the same age as you.

Birthday _____

Name _____

Watches TV.

_____

Favorite program

_____

Name

Is wearing tennis shoes.

Kind _____

Name _____

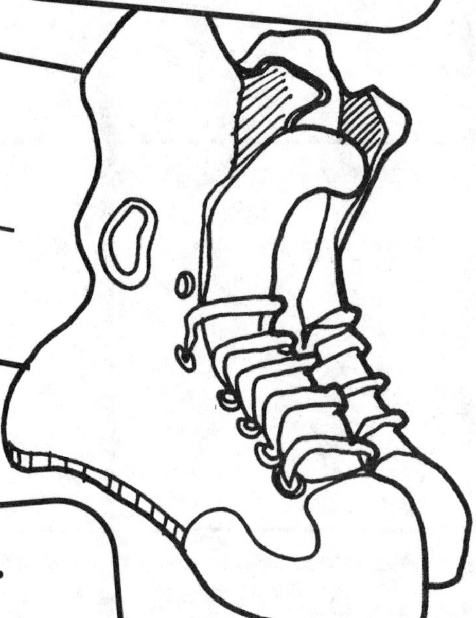

Was born in the summer.

Month _____

Name _____

Eats junk food.

_____

What type of food

_____

Name

Is wearing earings.

Where did you get them _____

Name _____

Find Someone Who...

Likes Movies.

_____

Favorite movie

_____

Name

Walks to school.

How long does it take _____

Name _____

Likes to eat pizza.

What toppings _____

Name _____

Has a pet.

_____

What kind of pet

_____

Name

Has been to the circus.

When _____

Name _____

Is wearing blue jeans.

What kind _____

Name _____

Find Someone Who...
can name a state.

Find Someone Who...
can name a continent or ocean.

People Hunt

Step 1: Fill in all of your preferences under "Self."

Step 2: Find someone similar to you & write their name in "Friend."

	Self	Friend
1. Favorite Color		
2. Favorite School Subject		
3. Favorite Ice Cream Flavor		
4. Birthday Month		
5. Favorite TV Show		
6. Eye Color		
7. Hobby		
8. Favorite Group		
9. I Want to Be...		
10. Favorite Food		
11. Favorite Drink		
12. Hair Color		
13. Dream Car		
14. Favorite Season		
15. Favorite Athlete		
16. Favorite Actor		
17. Favorite Movie		
18. Favorite Book		
19. Most fun Recess Game		
20. Favotie Cartoon		

People Hunt

	Self	Friend
1.		
2.		
3.		
4.		
5.		
6.		
7.		
8.		
9.		
10.		
11.		
12.		
13.		
14.		
15.		
16.		
17.		
18.		
19.		
20.		

Fact Bingo

Has Green Eyes	Has Brown hair	Wearing a T-Shirt	Has Brown Eyes	Wearing a Necklace
Wearing Red	Has 4 Pockets	Has Contact Lenses on	Wearing Blue Jeans	3 or More Buttons
Wearing Earings	Has Black Hair	FREE SPACE	Has Freckles	Has Blue Eyes
Wearing Blue	Wears Glasses	Has a Watch on	Tennis Shoes	Wearing Black Shoes
Has Curly Hair	Wearing Velcro	Walked to School	Has Blond Hair	Wearing a Ring

Fact Bingo

___	___	___	___	___
___	___	___	___	___
___	___	FREE SPACE	___	___
___	___	___	___	___
___	___	___	___	___

Formations

Students silently signal each other into position as they excitedly coordinate efforts to sculpt a challenging class formation.

In Formations, the teacher presents the class with something to form—like the capital letter "A" or the solar system. Students then make the formation by coordinating their efforts, deciding where each student should stand. More advanced formations include sound and movement. In a model for the solar system, the earth rotates around the sun and the moon rotates around the earth. A train formation is not complete without all class members chanting in unison: "Chug-a-chug-a-choo-choo!"

Formations serves as a class energizer at any point in a lesson because students are up and moving. Formations has a positive impact on classmate relations and class identity because students all work together to reach the class goal.

1 Teacher Announces Formation

The teacher directs the class to hold hands or stand to form a shape. The teacher may show the students a picture of the shape, or may give the instructions orally. "Form a capital letter 'A' by standing as a class in the shape of one large capital 'A.'"

② Students Create Formation

As a class, students work together to become the formation. Students position themselves in the classroom to stand in one large capital letter "A."

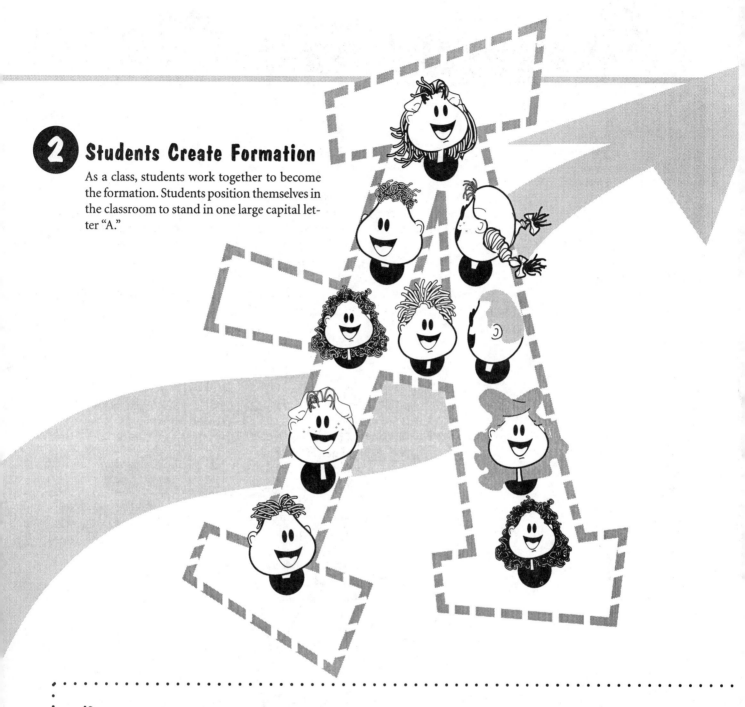

Hints

★ **Open Space.** If possible, take students to an open space such as a playing field, gym, or cafeteria.
★ **Use Visuals.** Show students a picture of the shape they are to form.
★ **Everyone Participates.** Tell the class the formation must involve all students.
★ **Increase Difficulty.** Start with easier formations and move to more complex ones. Do a circle before a hexagon.
★ **Model the Process.** Model how students may interact to make the formation.
★ **Links.** Give students one large piece of string tied in a circle, or many rubber bands linked together. All students hold on to the string or band as they create the formation.

Benefits

• All students are actively involved in creating the formation. • Students develop a concrete conceptual image of the formation created. • Kinesthetic learners receive input in their preferred modality. • Students coordinate efforts to succeed. • The class accomplishes a class goal.

Ideas for My Class!

Classbuilding

- Ice cream cone
- Class name
- Student name
- Grade level
- School name
- Balloon
- Hat
- Pencil
- Shoe
- Cookie
- Pair of glasses
- Article of clothing
- Pizza
- Keyboard

Mathematics

- Geometric figures
- Numbers (1, 5, 9, 13)
- Operations (+, -, X, ÷)
- Shapes
- Number sentences (8+1=9)
- Algebraic equation
- People graphs
- Patterns (tallest to shortest)
- Fractions
- Number groups

Variations

Card Formations Give each student a card with something written on it such as a letter. Students make the formation based on the content of their cards. In this case, students could line up where the letter is found on the keyboard.

Team Formations Give each team a formation to create. Have the rest of the class try to guess what the formation is.

Silent Formations Make Formations more challenging and have students participate more equally by announcing a rule: No talking while creating the formation.

Picture Formations Cut a picture into the number of students there are in the class. Each student gets a portion of the picture. The task is for students to position themselves to recreate the picture. If each student is given part of the Eiffel Tower some students will be responsible for the base and others for the tower.

Advanced Formations Make the formations more elaborate by using objects in the classroom as visual aids. Students may use the PE equipment (balls, jump ropes, bats) to form a skeleton or chairs for the seats in the space shuttle. Make the class come alive by having formations that require movement and sound.

Principles

Positive Interdependence Students need each other; no individual can create the formation alone.

Individual Accountability Each student is accountable to the class for making a visible contribution to the formation.

Equal Participation Students are equal participants in the formation.

Simultaneous Interaction All students interact at once as they create the formation.

Science

• Tree
• Fish
• Solar System
• Parts of a plant
• Land formations
• Animals
• Water cycle
• Dinosaur
• Simple machine
• Chemicals (H20)
• Elements in Periodic Table
• Chemical reactions
• Parts of an airplane
• Skeletal structure
• Digestive system
• Body parts

Social Studies

• Flag
• Covered wagon
• Words
• Shape state
• Spell city live in
• President's name
• Geographical formations
• States
• Countries
• Seas
• Rivers
• Mountains

Language Arts

• Letters: upper and lower case
• Book
• Abbreviations
• Words
• Scene of a story
• Parts of sentences
• Punctuation

Formations

Formation Cards: Shapes

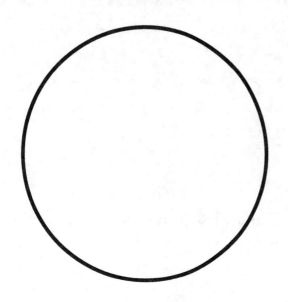

Circle

Square

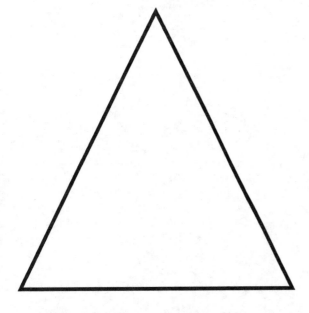

Triangle

Star

Formation Cards: Shapes

Heart

Balloon

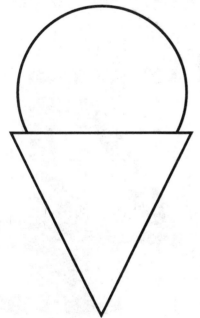

Ice Cream

House

Formation Cards: Numbers

1

2

3

4

Formation Cards: Numbers

5

6

7

8

Formation Cards: Letters

A

B

C

D

Formation Cards: Letters

R   S

Y   Z

Formation Cards: Punctuation

Formation Cards: Punctuation

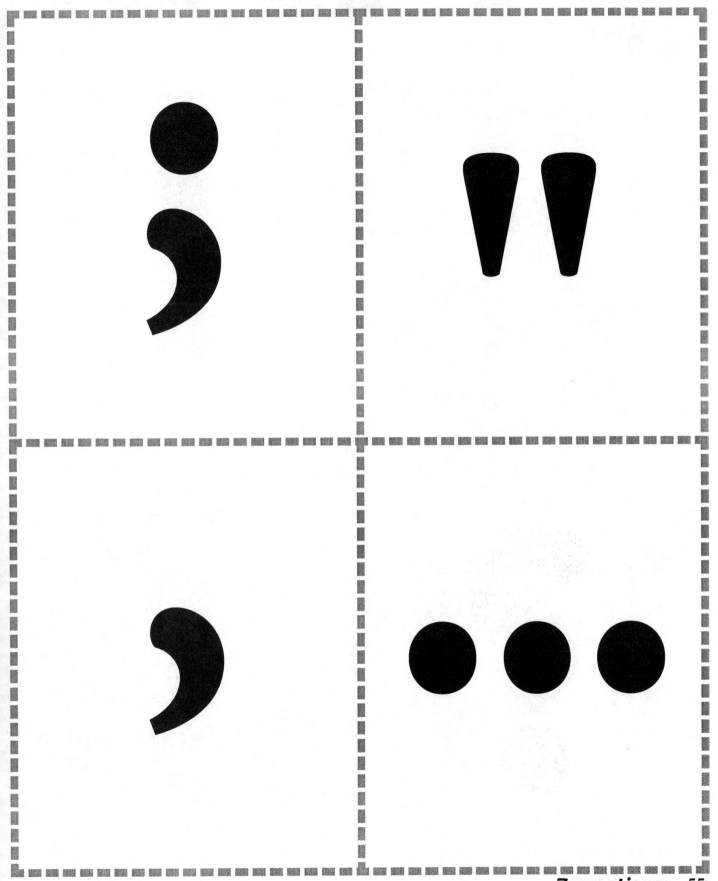

Guess-the-Fib

The class becomes a game show as students sharpen their wits, have some healthy laughs, and learn little known facts about classmates.

In Guess-the-Fib each student writes down three statements. Two of the statements are true and one is a fib. One student at a time leads the class. The student reads his/her three statements to the class. Teams huddle to discuss the statements, trying to "guess the fib." If most teams guess the fib, the student applauds the class; if not, the class applauds the student.

Guess-the-Fib is good for getting acquainted and for learning more personal information about classmates. Because Guess-the-Fib is a fun game for the entire class; it fosters a positive classroom climate.

1 Students Write Three Statements

Have each student write three statements. "We are going to play Guess-the-Fib, so everyone needs to come up with three statements about themselves. Two of the statements are unbelievable facts and one statement is a believable fib."

2 One Student Reads Statements

One student is randomly selected to read his/her statements to the class.

GUESS

4 Teammates Guess

The student presenting the statement asks how many teams guessed statements one, two, and three. Teams respond by holding up a slate or showing one, two, or three fingers. Teams which did not reach consensus do not respond.

Play again: The class repeats steps two through four so that a number of students present their statements.

3 Teammates Discuss Statements

Teams put their heads together to reach consensus on which one of the three statements is the fib. "Put your heads together as a team and decide together which one is the fib. For your team to vote you must reach consensus."

Hints

★ **Team Consensus.** Have teams reach consensus: Its easier to count teams than individuals, plus teams get practice reaching consensus.

★ **Fact-or-Fiction.** Fact-or-Fiction is easier for younger students than Guess-the-Fib. See Variations.

★ **Make Corrections.** Make sure students correct the fib so students remember correct information.

★ **Consensus Skills.** Teach teams that consensus seeking is a skill. It involves "give and take." "When you reach consensus, your job is not to get your way, it is to make sure your team has an answer everyone feels comfortable with."

★ **Consensus Seeker.** Have a rotating role within teams of "Consensus Seeker" to help reach consensus.

Benefits

• Students learn to take the role of others, second guessing how others will think. • Students become comfortable sharing personal information. • Students get acquainted, learning more about classmates. • Teams learn to reach consensus.

Ideas for My Class!

Classbuilding

- Personal events
- What I did today
- What I did yesterday
- What I will do tomorrow
- Personal Facts
- Things I enjoy
- Things I can't stand
- About my family
- About my friends
- Classroom procedures
- Class rules
- Conflict resolution

Mathematics

- Answers to problems
- Measurement equations
- Properties of geometrical shapes
- Steps in a proof
- Next in a pattern
- Probability of an event
- Graphs which follow data
- Points on a plane
- Numbers greater, equal, less than
- Odd or even
- Concave or convex
- Symmetrical or asymmetrical

Team Guess-the-Fib Each team comes up with three statements about the team or its members. In this version, teams rather than individuals are coming up with statements.

Playing for Points Students or teams can play for points to add friendly competition. Students earn points for how many teams they fool; teams earn points for how many fibs they find.

Fact-or-Fiction Students state either a believable lie or an unlikely truth. Classmates attempt to guess if it is fact or fiction. For example, a student might state, "George Washington had wooden teeth which he had trouble controlling."

Guess How Many Fibs To make the game more challenging for older students, either one, two, or three of the statements may be fibs.

Response Modes

Thumbs Up, Thumbs Down Individuals can vote with their thumbs — thumbs up for a true statement or Fact; thumbs down for a fib or Fiction.

Finger Responses Students signal their guess by holding up one, two, or three fingers.

Card Responses Students hold up cards with the number corresponding to the fib.

Principles

Positive Interdependence If one student on a team can provide correct information it helps the team reach correct consensus. Teams want other teams to do well as it helps the class Guess-the-Fib.

Individual Accountability Students selected are accountable for sharing statements with the class.

Equal Participation Students participate equally in coming up with the three statements.

Simultaneous Interaction Students come up with statements at the same time. One quarter of the class is active at once during the team discussion.

Science

- Classifying animals
- Identifying animals
- Plausible inferences from data
- Procedures in experiment
- Observations of specimen
- Location of organs
- Parts of a system
- Function of organs
- Location of planets
- Name of scientists
- Scientist's findings

Social Studies

- Amendments
- Character traits of historical characters
- Dates of events
- Actions of historical characters
- Time zones of places
- Location of states
- Characteristics of various groups
- Job descriptions
- Capitals of states
- Sequence of events
- Causes of events
- Structure of government
- Events at a place

Language Arts

- Reading comprehension
- Parts of speech
- Cause and effect
- Determine the plot
- Main idea of a story
- Theme
- Conflict in a story
- Actions of characters
- Facts about characters

Guess-the-Fib

News Travels Fast

1. I Like

_____

2. I Like

_____

3. I Like

_____

Name _____

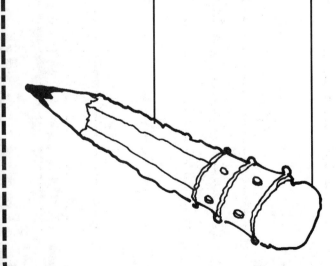

A WHALE OF A TALE!

PRESENTED BY

Just the Fax

TRANSMITTED BY _____

1 _____
_____
_____

2 _____
_____
_____

3 _____
_____
_____

Hear Ye! Hear Ye!

Write one statement.

NAME

TRUE OR FALSE

Inside/Outside Circle

Students stand in anticipation, waiting for the teacher to call a number. They prepare to rotate, wondering which classmate will be their next partner for sharing or problem solving.

For Inside-Outside Circle, students form two concentric circles. Both circles have the same number of students. Students in the inside circle each face a student in the outside circle. The teacher announces a topic or question, and students discuss with their partners. Then, the teacher has both circles rotate so they are facing a new partner to discuss the same or a new topic.

Inside-Outside Circle is a great structure for having students share information with any classmate in an exciting way.

1 Students Form Circles

Students stand in two concentric circles around the classroom. Students in the inside circle face out, facing a partner standing in the outside circle. "We are going to do Inside-Outside Circle. First form one circle around the room facing in. Next, half of you move to the inside and turn to face a partner who is standing in the outside circle. If you do not find a partner, hold up a hand so others will find you."

2 Student Shares with Partner

Have students from the inside circle share something with their partners. "Inside circle students discuss what you did this Saturday afternoon with your partner. You have one minute."

③ Reverse Roles

Students switch roles; the outside circle students now share while their partners listen. "Outside circle students, its your turn to share for a minute."

④ Students Rotate

Have students rotate to work with new partners. "Everyone in the class face your partner. Now, make a right face and count out loud as you all rotate four people ahead to a new partner."

Repeat: Students discuss different topics each time they rotate to different partners.

H i n t s

★ **Play Outside.** If it is a nice day, bring the class outside to enjoy Inside-Outside Circle.
★ **Vary Rotating.** To spice up rotating, vary the number of positions advanced and occasionally switch the direction of rotation.
★ **Choral Counting.** Have the class count out loud the number of positions they are moving so everyone knows when to stop. "One, two, THREE!"

Benefits

• Students problem solve or share with many partners. • Students hear multiple perspectives. • When the content is review or problem solving, the class attempts to make sure everyone knows. • Movement energizes students.

Ideas for My Class!

Classbuilding

• Did this weekend
• Favorite restaurant and what order
• Favorite movie, why
• Favorite subject, why
• Favorite sport/hobby, how often
• Favorite color, why
• Favorite season, why
• Favorite month, why
• Favorite car, why
• Would rather be, explain why
• Preferred vacation spot, why

Mathematics

• Basic operations
• Telling time
• Story problems
• Reducing fractions
• Name shapes
• Name next item in pattern
• Name money
• Measure item
• Extend number pattern
• Distinguish shapes
• Identify angles
• Multiplication facts

Variations

Pair Inside-Outside Circle Have students rotate in pairs and discuss in groups of four. A typical sequence might be: 1) teacher asks a question; 2) inside circle pair discusses question while outside circle discusses question; 3) pairs compare answers.

Student Generated Questions Let students come up with questions they want to ask other students in the classroom. Put the questions in a hat and draw out one question each time the circles rotate.

Flashcards Have each student make up one question on a flashcard. Students ask each other their questions and switch cards before each rotation. With each rotation, students get a new partner and a new question. The teacher can supply the flashcards, or act as a quality control filter by collecting and correcting the cards before they are used.

Positive Interdependence Student thinking is enriched by hearing the ideas of many classmates.

Individual Accountability Students are accountable to their partner for sharing.

Equal Participation All students discuss and share equally.

Simultaneous Interaction Students discuss in pairs, so that half of the the class is speaking at a time.

Science

• Vocabulary
• Parts of animal
• Parts of plants
• Types of rocks
• Types of dinosaurs
• Name body parts
• Classify animals
• Identify cloud types
• Functions of organs
• Functions of systems
• Identify elements
• Identify animals
• Predict outcomes

Social Studies

• Name state capitals
• Name the country
• Recognize famous explorers
• Name Bill of Rights
• Explaining an Amendment
• Describe the function of branch
• Identify peoples
• Identify customs
• Locate states on map
• Locate country on map
• Name the place of the event
• List contributions of individuals
• Be historical character, why
• Participate in historical event, why
• Live in what country, why
• Preferred profession, why

Language Arts

• Predict ending of story
• Recall the events of story
• Vocabulary words
• Spelling words
• Parts of speech
• Generate ideas for prewriting
• Favorite book, why
• Favorite character, why
• Describe action of character
• Discuss a reading

• Share a story
• Share a poem
• Share a book report
• Peer editing
• Identify the author
• Distinguish writing type
• Identify story structure
• Simile or metaphor
• Persuade partner of position
• Recall story

Inside/Outside Circle

QUESTION CARDS: ALL ABOUT SCHOOL

1 What is your favorite subject in school? What do you like best about it?

2 What is your favorite activity at recess? What do you like best about it?

3 Who is the best teacher you ever had? Why is he or she the best ever?

4 If you could make the school schedule, when would you have school start, recess, lunch, stop?

5 If you were the teacher, what would you do differently? Why?

6 If you could be in any grade you wanted, what grade would you be? Explain your answer.

7 What is your least favorite subject in school? What don't you like about it?

8 Name three things that would make you a better student. Would you want to change?

9 Name three things that would make this a better school.

10 Finish this statement. Right after school, I am going to _____

11 Do you prefer year round or do you prefer long summer vacations? Why?

12 What is the best thing about this class. Explain your answer.

13 Name two ways you could help the teacher?

14 What is one thing the teacher could do to make this class better?

15 Who is your best friend in this class? Why are you best friends?

16 Finish this statement. School is _____

1 If you could be an animal for one day, what animal would you be? Why did you select this animal?

2 Do you have any brothers or sisters? How old are they?

3 What do you want to be when you grow up? Explain your answer.

4 What is your favorite sport or hobby? How often do you do it?

5 What is your favorite TV program? What do you like about it?

6 If you could jump into any book, what book would it be? Why did you select this book?

7 If you could be anyone for a week, who would it be? Explain why.

8 What is the best present you ever received? When did you get it? Why is it the best?

9 Name three things that make you unique.

10 If you were on a deserted island and could only have three things with you, what would they be?

11 If you rubbed a magic lamp and a genie said he would grant you three wishes, what would they be?

12 What is the most exciting thing you have ever done? Why was it so exciting?

13 If you could go anywhere in the world on vacation, where would you go? Explain why.

14 If you could get in a time machine, what time period and where would you visit? Why?

15 Who is the most important person or persons in your life? Why are they so important?

16 Finish these statements:
I am _____
My favorite _____
I would like _____

QUESTION CARDS: MORE ABOUT ME

1 If you could change one thing about yourself, what would it be?

2 Where do you see yourself in twenty-five years?

3 What was the most embarrassing thing that ever happened to you?

4 What was one thing that made your parents very proud of you?

5 What is the most difficult thing you have ever done?

6 What is the most fun you ever had?

7 What is the biggest mistake you ever made?

8 What is the best practical joke you ever played on anyone?

9 If you could be invisible for a whole day, what would you do?

10 Describe a time when you felt like a million bucks.

11 What is the funniest thing that ever happened to you?

12 Describe the scariest situation you have ever been in.

13 Do you have a nickname that you like to be called? How did you get it?

14 Tell about a time when you got into a whole lot of trouble. What did you do and why did you do it?

15 Describe your favorite dinner.

16 What are your top three treasured possessions and why?

1 If you were killed in a car accident, would you want to donate your organs to help someone else?

2 If you could cheat on a test and get a good grade and never be caught, would you do it?

3 If a spaceship landed in your backyard and said I will take you to Mars, but you can never come back, would you go?

4 If you were told you would never have to work a day in your life, would you still work?

5 If you could look into a crystal ball and see the future, but couldn't change it, would you do it?

6 Your grandmother makes you a sweater, and you can't stand it. Do you wear it for her?

7 The cashier gives you twenty dollars too much change. Do you tell her?

8 If you could take a drug to make you smarter, would you take it?

9 If you found a wallet without identification and three hundred dollars, would you turn it in or keep it?

10 If you could rob a bank and get away with it, would you do it?

11 Would you rather be attractive and dumb or unattractive and smart?

12 Would you rather be a famous actor or come up with the cure for cancer?

13 If you saw a really poor person steal food in the grocery store, would you turn them in?

14 Your mother is dying of a rare disease. The only way to get the medicine is to steal it. What do you do?

15 You can kill an evil dictator and save the lives of thousands, but go to jail for life. What do you do?

16 Your best friend lies to the teacher. The teacher says he is in big trouble if it is a lie and asks you if it is a lie. What do you do.

Question Cards: What Do You Think

1 Is it important to marry someone of the same religion as you?

2 Should scientists do testing on live animals?

3 Do you think motorcyclists should be required by law to wear a helmet? How about a seat belt?

4 Should guns be illegal? Explain why or why not.

5 Do you think we should have capital punishment? Explain why or why not.

6 Do you think you have control of your actions, or are your actions somehow determined?

7 Do you believe there is life on another planet?

8 Do you think some people have extrasensory perception (ESP)? Why or why not?

9 Do you think that the rich should be taxed more than the poor, or should everyone be taxed the same? Explain your answer.

10 Should abortion be legal? Describe your position.

11 Do you think groups should be allowed to publicly demonstrate even if they are spreading hate?

12 Do you believe in life after death?

13 Do you believe that after you die you are reincarnated?

14 What is more important: Domestic or foreign affairs.

15 What is more important: Space exploration or solving pollution problems. Why?

16 Do you believe in ghosts? Explain your answer.

1
You are the author of a new best-selling book. What is the book about?

2
You have just invented a new flavor of ice cream. What flavor is it?

3
You've got a great new solution to end pollution. What is it?

4
Your class needs to raise two hundred dollars to go on a field trip. What is your suggestion?

5
If the doctor told you that you only had six months longer to live, what would you do?

6
What would you do if you went into your basement and found a time machine?

7
You've just heard a hilarious but clean joke, what is it?

8
You've just invented a brand new sport and everyone loves to play. What is your sport called and how do you play?

9
You just got elected President. What do you do now?

10
You have just painted a masterpiece. What is it and what does it look like?

11
You just came up with a fabulous new dish. What is it and what are the ingredients?

12
Everyone is talking about the new movie you directed. What is it about? Who are the actors?

13
Your new band is topping the charts. What is the name of your band and what type of music do you play?

14
You just came back from a brand new amusement park. It's the best one you've ever been to. Describe it.

15
You've just invented a brand new vitamin. What is it and what does it do?

16
You've just come up with an alternative form of energy. Scientists everywhere want to know about it.

Line-Ups

Students find they each occupy a unique position in the class and the class can see at a glance where everyone stands.

In Line-Ups, the teacher announces a dimension upon which students may vary. The dimension may either be a characteristic like "How large is our big thumb? or a value like, "Do we agree or disagree with capital punishment?" Students then line-up according to where they stand relative to their classmates on the characteristic or issue.

Line-Ups is a very strong structure for having students clarify their own stance as well as for having classmates appreciate individual differences. Line-Ups promotes a process through which students hear perspectives different from their own. Students come to not only accept, but value diversity. Line-Ups establishes a continuum rather than poles, moving students away from "either-or" thinking toward more differentiated thinking.

2 **Students Line Up**

Students position themselves in the line-up by finding where they stand relative to their classmates.

1 **Teacher Describes the Line**

Announce a dimension upon which students vary. "Line up by height from shortest to tallest."

③ Pairs Discuss

Students pair up with the student next to them to discuss. "Would you like to be taller or shorter? What do you like best and least about your height?"

Ideas for My Class!

Classbuilding

- Height
- Number of buttons wearing
- Shoe size
- Birthday
- Number of pets
- Number of syllables in names
- Number of minutes takes to get to school
- Distance from school
- Time went to bed
- Time woke up
- Number of brothers or sisters
- Number of letters in name
- Birth order

Mathematics

- Number order
- Decimal order
- Fraction order
- Percent order
- Value of money
- Angle size
- Area of shape
- Volume of container
- Answer to word problem
- Length of string
- Written number
- Remainder in division

Variations

Value Line-Ups
Students line up relative to their classmates based on where they stand on an issue. The poles are usually agree/disagree or like/dislike. For example have students line up on the statement: "Math is more fun than Language Arts."

Sequencing Line-Ups
Line-Ups can be used to have students sequence events. Give each student a card with a letter or number and then line up in sequence.

Folded Line-Ups
The value line-up can be folded to have students with different characteristics or values meet and discuss. To fold the line-up, have the students at one end of the line walk over to the other end. Students follow the leader so that when they stop, each is across from a new partner. New partners shake hands and discuss the issue.

Share & Fold
Before folding a Value Line, have students first discuss the issue with a partner next to them in the line up. This provides students support for their stance as well as arming them with better ideas to share with their new partner after the Value Line is folded.

Split & Slide Line-Ups
The line-up is split in the middle. Half of the line takes three steps forward. The line then slides down so that every student faces another student. Students who were in the middle of the line-up are now faced with students from the ends. After the split and slide, students discuss with their partner topics provided by the teacher.

Paraphrase Passport
In Folded Value Line-Ups, students discuss issues with students of different viewpoints. To validate what the other student is saying, play Paraphrase Passport. Students must paraphrase what their partner said before speaking. Paraphrasing promotes listening skills because students know they must listen if they are to paraphrase.

Praise Passport
Praise Passport is the same as paraphrase passport except students must praise something their partner said before speaking. Students feel that their perspective is worthy when it is appreciated. Praise Passport makes students look for virtues in a perspective different from their own. Remind students that they do not have to agree with a point of view to appreciate how well it is stated, the thought which went into it, or the strength of the feelings behind it.

Principles

Positive Interdependence Students' ideas are enriched when they share with students who are like them and different from them.

Individual Accountability Students are accountable to their partners for sharing. Paraphrase Passport holds students accountable for listening.

Equal Participation Students have equal time to share and listen.

Simultaneous Interaction Students are in pairs so half the class is discussing at once.

Science

• Life cycles
• Water cycles
• Plant growth
• Stages in development
• Order of items by weight
• Order of items by size
• Order of items by height
• Order of items by volume
• Steps in procedures
• Steps in process
• Order animals by speed
• Order machines by speed
• Moral issues in science
• Stance on euthanasia
• Stance on animal experimentation

Social Studies

• Timeline
• Sequence of events
• Life of historical characters
• Steps in passing a bill
• Steps in election process
• Famous person's life sequence
• States in alphabetical order
• Inventions in order
• President in order
• Amendments in order
• Position on moral issues
• Stance on abortion
• Stance on capital punishment
• Stance on health care
• Stance on welfare
• Stance on environmental issues

Language Arts

• Alphabetical order of word
• Alphabetical order of letters
• Alphabetical order of author
• Events of a story
• Number of characters in story
• Stance on literature
• Like or dislike a story
• Like or dislike an author
• Like or dislike a play or skit
• Agree or disagree with editorial
• Agree or disagree with author
• Believe or disbelieve story

Line-Ups

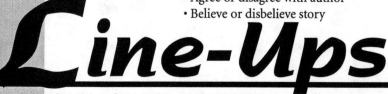

 AGREE

 NOT SURE

 DISAGREE

YES

MAYBE

NO

FOR

NOT SURE

AGAINST

 LIKE

 NOT SURE

 DISLIKE

Line-Ups
Sequence the Numbers

1	2	3	4
5	6	7	8
9	10	11	12
13	14	15	16

Line-Ups
Sequence the Numbers

17	18	19	20
21	22	23	24
25	26	27	28
29	30	31	32

ABC Line-Ups
Sequence the Letters

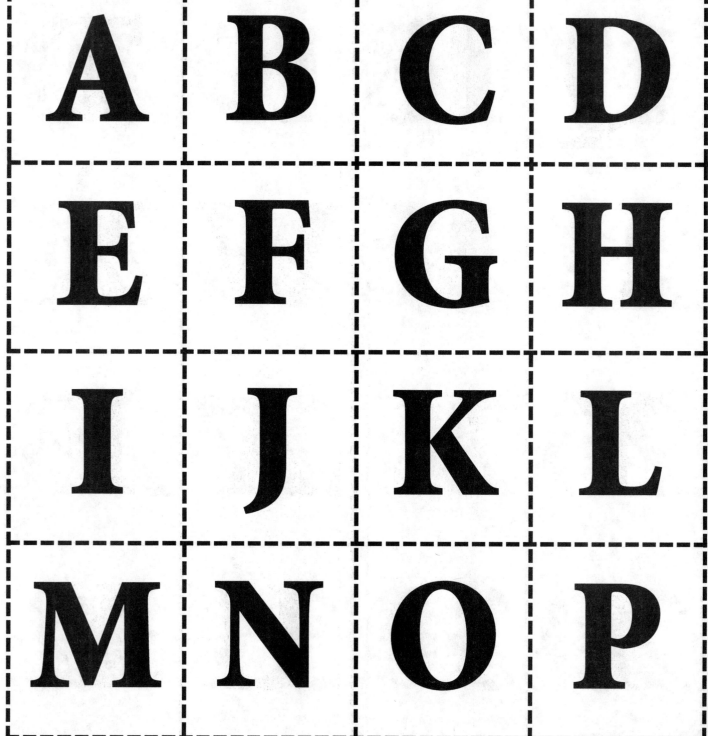

A	B	C	D
E	F	G	H
I	J	K	L
M	N	O	P

ABC Line-Ups XYZ
Sequence the Letters

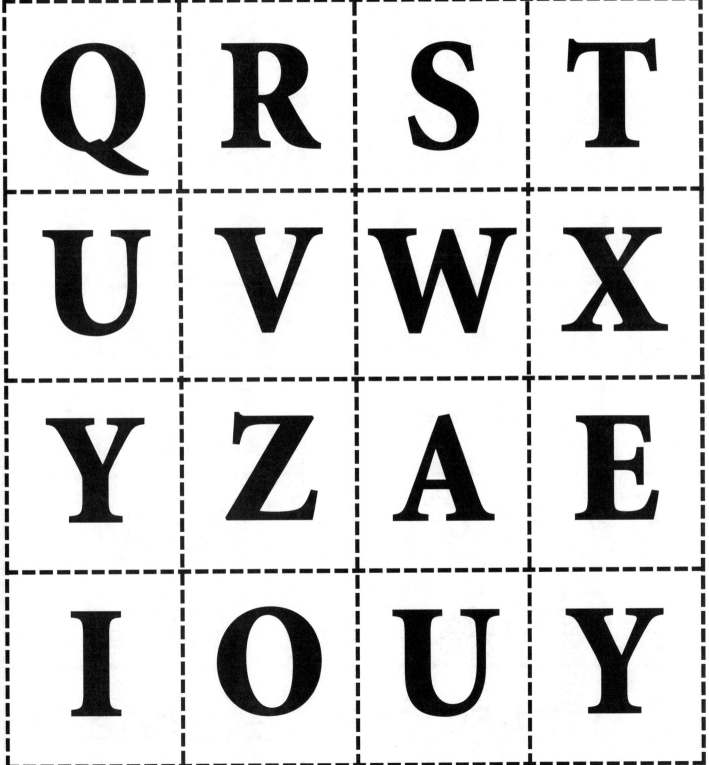

ABC Line-Ups
Alphabetize the Words

Apple	Igloo
Bell	Jacket 
Car	Kangaroo
 Desk	Lamb
Elf	Mouse 
 Fish	Noisy
Giraffe	Owl
House	Parade

ABC Line-Ups

Alphabetize the Words

Quarter	Zoo
Roasted	Amazing
Shoe 	Bee
Television	Canada
Umbrella	Deer
Very	Ear
 Whale	Funny
Xylophone	Goat

Line-Ups
Fun with Fractions

Line-Ups
Fun with Fractions

Line-Ups

Sequence the Presidents

George Washington	William Henry Harrison
John Adams	John Tyler
Thomas Jefferson	James Knox Polk
James Madison	Zachary Taylor
James Monroe	Millard Fillmore
John Quincy Adams	Franklin Pierce
Andrew Jackson	James Buchanan
Martin Van Buren	Abraham Lincoln

Line-Ups

Sequence the Presidents

Andrew Johnson	William McKinley
Ulysses Simpson Grant	Theodore Roosevelt
Rutherford Birchard Hayes	William Howard Taft
James Abram Garfield	Thomas Woodrow Wilson
Chester Alan Arthur	Warren Gamaliel Harding
Stephen Grover Clevland	John Calvin Coolidge
Benjamin Harrison	Herbert Clark Hoover
Stephen Grover Cleveland	Franklin Delano Roosevelt

Line-Ups

Sequence the Presidents

Harry S. Truman	George Herbert Walker Bush
Dwight David Eisenhower	William Clinton
John Fitzgerald Kennedy	
Lyndon Baines Johnson	
Richard Milhous Nixon	
Gerald Rudolf Ford	
Jimmy Carter	
Ronald Reagan	

Presidents in Order

1. George Washington 1789-1797

2. John Adams 1797-1801

3. Thomas Jefferson 1801-1809

4. James Madison 1809-1817

5. James Monroe 1817-1825

6. John Quincy Adams 1825-1829

7. Andrew Jackson 1829-1837

8. Martin Van Buren 1837-1841

9. William Henry Harrison 1841

10. John Tyler 1841-1845

11. James Knox Polk 1845-1849

12. Zachary Taylor 1849-1850

13. Millard Fillmore 1850-1853

14. Franklin Pierce 1853-1857

15. James Buchanan 1857-1861

16. Abraham Lincoln 1861-1865

17. Andrew Johnson 1865-1869

18. Ulysses Simpson Grant 1869-1877

19. Rutherford Birchard Hayes 1877-1881

20. James Abram Garfield 1881

21. Chester Alan Arthur 1881-1885

22. Stephen Grover Clevland 1885-1889

23. Benjamin Harrison 1889-1893

Stephen Grover Cleveland 1893-1897

24. William McKinley 1897-1901

25. Theodore Roosevelt 1901-1909

26. William Howard Taft 1909-1913

27. Thomas Woodrow Wilson 1913-1921

28. Warren Gamaliel Harding 1921-1923

29. John Calvin Coolidge 1923-1929

30. Herbert Clark Hoover 1929-1933

31. Franklin Delano Roosevelt 1933-1945

32. Harry S. Truman 1945-1953

33. Dwight David Eisenhower 1953-1961

34. John Fitzgerald Kennedy 1961-1963

35. Lyndon Baines Johnson 1963-1969

36. Richard Milhous Nixon 1969-1974

37. Gerald Rudolf Ford 1974-1977

38. Jimmy Carter 1977-1981

39. Ronald Reagan 1981-1989

40. George Herbert Walker Bush 1989-1993

41. William Clinton 1993-Present

Line-Ups
Sequence Cinderella

Cinderella's stepsisters make her work day and night.	The Fairy Godmother waves her wand.
Cinderella asked her stepsisters if she could go to the ball with them.	The Fairy Godmother turns a pumpkin into a coach and Cinderella's dress into a gown.
Cinderella's stepsisters would not let her go to the ball with them.	After Cinderella is ready for the ball, she is warned that she must leave before midnight.
Cinderella cried as her stepsisters left in the carriage for the ball without her.	Cinderella hops into the coach and is off to the ball.
After her stepsisters leave, Cinderella wishes she could also go to the ball.	Cinderella arrives at the palace and goes into the ball.
Cinderella's Fairy Godmother appears.	In the ball, everyone asks who is the beautiful girl with the glass slippers.
Cinderella's Fairy Godmother tells her that she will grant her the wish of going to the ball.	The Prince notices Cinderella.
Cinderella tells her Fairy Godmother that she has no coach and no clothes.	Cinderella and the Prince dance all evening long.

Line-Ups
Sequence Cinderella

The clock begins to chime twelve.	The men search everywhere for the owner of the glass slipper.
Cinderella leaves the Prince and runs out of the ball.	Finally, the men come to the house of Cinderella and her stepsisters.
The spell ends. Cinderella's coach is again a pumkin and her gown again a ragged dress.	Cinderella's stepsisters try on the slipper.
The Prince runs out of the ball and looks for Cinderella.	The slipper does not fit on the stepsisters' feet.
The Prince cannot find Cinderella anywhere.	The footman tells the stepsisters to bring out Cinderella.
The Prince spots a glass slipper on the steps.	The Prince tries the slipper on Cinderella's foot.
The Prince says he will marry the owner of the slipper.	It is a perfect fit!
The Prince orders a search for the owner of the glass slipper.	Cinderella and the Prince get married and live happily ever after.

Line-Ups
Sequence the Political Events

Boston Tea Party in the Boston Harbor. It was one of the events that led to the Revolutionary War.

President Lincoln gave the Gettysburg Address on the battlefield at Gettysburg, Pennsylvania, four months after the battle.

Revolutionary War fought by Americans against Great Britain.

Abraham Lincoln was shot and killed by John Wilkes Booth who supported slavery and the confederacy.

The Declaration of Independence was adopted by the thirteen colonies.

Civil Rights Act established Negroes as American citizens.

Constitution is written, with the help of Benjamin Franklin and others.

Congress passed the act, creating the Department of Justice.

The Mexican War begins. It is fought at the Alamo and resulted in the U.S. gaining territory in the Southwest.

The Sioux Indians, led by Sitting Bull, fought against Custer at Little Bighorn, killing Custer and all his men.

The Confederacy seceded from the US to form a new nation.

The surrender of the Apache Geronimo put an end to "formal" warfare between Indians and whites.

The Civil War begins. It is fought between the North and South states.

World War I begins. At first, U.S. tried to stay neutral, but in 1917 took the side of Britain and France.

Lincoln issued the Emancipation Proclamation, which lead to the end of slavery.

The 18th Amendment is added which prohibited sale, manufacture or transportation of alcoholic beverages. Later it was repealed.

Line-Ups
Sequence the Political Events

19th Amendment guarantees women the right to vote.

Martin Luther King Jr. the civil rights activist is assassinated.

The Great Depression begins. It is the worst economic period in American history.

Vietnam War fought between South and North Vietnam ended when North Vietnam conquered South Vietnam.

President Franklin D. Roosevelt begins speaking directly to the American people by means of radio in "fireside chats."

U.S. access to Canal Zone given back to the Republic of Panama.

World War II begins.

First Lady, Nancy Reagan, initiates her war on drugs, with her "Just Say No" slogan.

Japanese planes made a surprise attack on Pearl Harbor naval base.

Iran returned the hostages to the U.S. after 14 months of negotiating on the same day Carter left office.

D-Day: The day that British and American troops invaded German-occupied France during World War II.

Iran-Contra Affair exposed, bringing Oliver North and President Reagan into the spotlight as key offenders.

Korean War ends during Eisenhower's presidency.

The Gulf War, known as "Operation Desert Storm," was fought in Kuwait and Iraq.

Civil Rights Act guaranteed equal rights for all people in public places, education and employment.

William Clinton is elected President. The first Democratic president in twelve years.

Political Events in Order

1773
Boston Tea Party in the Boston Harbor. It was one of the events that led to the Revolutionary War.

1774
Revolutionary War fought by Americans against Great Britain.

1776
The Declaration of Independence was adopted by the thirteen colonies.

1787
Constitution is written, with the help of Benjamin Franklin and others.

1846-1848
The Mexican War begins. It is fought at the Alamo and resulted in the U.S. gaining territory in the Southwest.

1860
The Confederacy seceded from the US to form a new nation.

1861-1865
The Civil War begins. It is fought between the North and South states.

1863
Lincoln issued the Emancipation Proclamation, which lead to the end of slavery.

1865
President Lincoln gave the Gettysburg Address on the battlefield at Gettysburg, Pennsylvania, four months after the battle.

1865
Abraham Lincoln was shot and killed by John Wilkes Booth who supported slavery and the confederacy.

1866
Civil Rights Act established Negroes as American citizens.

1870
Congress passed the act, creating the Department of Justice.

1876
The Sioux Indians, led by Sitting Bull, fought against Custer at Little Bighorn, killing Custer and all his men.

1886
The surrender of the Apache Geronimo put an end to "formal" warfare between Indians and whites.

1914-1918
World War I begins. At first, U.S. tried to stay neutral, but in 1917 took the side of Britain and France.

1919
The 18th Amendment is added which prohibited sale, manufacture or transportation of alcoholic beverages. Later it was repealed.

Political Events in Order

1920
19th Amendment guarantees women the right to vote.

1929-1938
The Great Depression begins. It is the worst economic period in American history.

1933
President Franklin D. Roosevelt begins speaking directly to the American people by means of radio in "fireside chats."

1939
World War II begins.

1941
Japanese planes made a surprise attack on Pearl Harbor naval base.

1944
D-Day: The day that British and American troops invaded German-occupied France during World War II.

1953
Korean War ends during Eisenhower's presidency.

1964
Civil Rights Act guaranteed equal rights for all people in public places, education and employment.

1968
Martin Luther King Jr. the civil rights activist is assassinated.

1975
Vietnam War fought between South and North Vietnam ended when North Vietnam conquered South Vietnam.

1978
U.S. access to Canal Zone given back to the Republic of Panama.

1980
First Lady, Nancy Reagan, initiates her war on drugs, with her "Just Say No" slogan.

1981
Iran returned the hostages to the U.S. after 14 months of negotiating on the same day Carter left office.

1988
Iran-Contra Affair exposed, bringing Oliver North and President Reagan into the spotlight as key offenders.

1990
The Gulf War, known as "Operation Desert Storm," was fought in Kuwait and Iraq.

1992
William Clinton is elected President. The first Democratic president in twelve years.

Mix-Freeze-Group

The classroom is bursting with energy as students rapidly "Mix" around the room, "Freeze" in their tracks, and frantically "Group" to avoid falling into the lost and found.

When the teacher announces to the class that they are going to play Mix-Freeze-Group, everyone gets out of their seat, pushes in their chair, and starts to circulate randomly about the classroom. Each student cruises around aimlessly until the teacher calls "Freeze." Students stop in their tracks and get ready to form a group. The size of the group depends on a clue from the teacher. The clue might be: "How many letters are there in the words 'Our Class?'" Students quickly answer the question mentally and scramble to form a group of eight by joining hands with their nearest classmates. Students know that if they don't join a group of the required size, they will become part of lost and found. The lost and found is all of the leftover students who stand in front of the classroom. Lost and found students are not excluded: as a rule, no student can be in the lost and found two rounds in a row.

Mix-Freeze-Group is a great energizer as all students are actively involved. Students are excited to play Mix-Freeze-Group, and the high level of excitement contributes to a positive class tone.

❶ Students "Mix"

Announce that students are to stand and push in their chairs. Then they are to "Mix." "We are going to play "Mix-Freeze-Group. Everyone get up and start to mix through the classroom. Make rapid right turns and left turns, and about faces. Spread out around the whole room. Keep moving until I call, "Freeze."

❷ Students "Freeze"

After students mix for a bit, call "Freeze." Students freeze exactly where they are.

3 Students "Group"

Provide a clue so students know the size group to form. Students rush to hold hands forming groups. "How many syllables are there in 'Spring Vacation?' Group!" Students rush to form groups of four (corresponding to the four syllables in "Spring Vacation.")

B e n e f i t s

• Students enjoy playing, enhancing the class tone. • Students sharpen their listening and thinking skills because they must hear the question, solve it mentally, and act quickly. • Students interact with many classmates. • Students feel needed and included by other classmates as classmates grab for them to complete their groups.

Ideas for My Class!

Classbuilding

- Our grade level
- Our room number
- Number of fish in the tank
- Time we have reading
- Time we eat lunch
- Time we get out
- Time we have recess
- Number of students born in January
- How many more boys than girls

Mathematics

- Number of claps (clap, clap, clap = 3)
- Addition (4+2=6)
- Subtraction (4-2=2)
- Multiplication (3x4=12)
- Division (16/4=4)
- Fractions (1/2 of 8 = 4)
- Number sentences (5+3-2+8= 14)
- Number placement (3246- Number in the tens place, ones place)
- Number of sides on two triangles
- Number of quarts in a gallon
- Number of inches in half a foot
- Number of cups in a quart
- Number of ounces in cup

<u>Key: Greater than 10 = 2 Less that 10 = 3 Equal to 10 = 4</u>

- Four plus five minus three times two is
- Seven and twenty one sevenths is
- I invested twenty dollars but lost a third of my investment

Variations

Mix-Freeze-Pair Students "Mix" and "Freeze" like usual. Instead of giving a clue, call "Pair." Students form pairs with the person closest to them. Pairs interview each other on the topic announced, or discuss a question posed by the teacher. This is effective for having students pair up with a different partner each time.

Lost and Found Announces Have students from the lost and found announce the next clue. You may provide them a list to choose from if they don't come up with a question on their own.

Principles

Positive Interdependence Students need classmates to form groups.
Individual Accountability Students are responsible for listening to the clue and coming up with an answer.
Equal Participation Students participate equally.
Simultaneous Interaction All students mix, freeze and group at the same time.

Science

• Number of planets in the solar system (9)
• Number of planets are from the sun (Earth=3)
• Number of moons for a certain planet
• Number of hydrogen molecules in water (2)
• Number of legs on a spider
Key: Carnivore = 2 Herbivore = 3 Omnivore = 4
• A T-Rex is (2)
• Humans are (4)
• A giraffe is (3)

Social Studies

• Number of boats sailed with the Mayflower
• Which amendment is the Freedom of Speech
• Number of senators to a state (2)
• Number of continents
• Number of years for each presidential term (4)
• How many states start with "C"
• How many states touch the Pacific
• How many states border California
• How many amendments in the Bill of Rights
• How many original colonies were there
• Number of provinces in Canada
Key: North = 2 South = 3 East = 4 West = 5
• Oregon is_____of California (2)
• Brazil is in_____America (3)

Language Arts

Number of...
• Dwarfs in Snow White (7)
• Men in Rub Dub Dub (2)
• Blind Mice (3)
• Number of letters in a spelling word (Class= 13)
• Number of syllables (Cinderella=4)
• Number of nouns (verbs, adjectives, pronouns, adverbs) in the sentence (The cat sat on the chair = 2)
• Key .=2 !=3 ?=4
• Did you get my letter? (4)
• Look Out! (3)
• She is a friend of mine. (2)

Mix-Freeze-Group

A Day at the Zoo
P u n c t u a t i o n

KEY

- **.** = **2**
- **!** = **3**
- **?** = **4**
- **,** = **5**
- **"** = **6**
- **:** = **7**

1. We went to the zoo last weekend_
2. The zoo is a big_ exciting place.
3. We saw the following_ lions, tigers, bears, giraffes and zebras.
4. Is that a monkey_
5. "Right you are,_ said the zookeeper.
6. Did you see that tiger_
7. What huge teeth_
8. "Look_" cried my brother, pointing at the tiger.
9. If you're hungry_ we can go eat lunch.
10. For lunch, we ate hamburgers and fries_
11. After lunch_ we saw more animals.
12. Do you want to see the snakes_
13. My dad said, _We have to go home now."
14. What an exciting trip_
15. I want to go back really soon_

What's My Sign?

KEY	+ = 2	÷ = 4
	- = 3	x = 5

1. 3( )4 = 12

2. 2( )3 = 5

3. 8( )6 = 2

4. 20( )4 = 5

5. 16( )2 = 8

6. 7( )3 = 21

7. 5( )12 = 17

8. 3( )5 = 15

9. 12( )6 = 6

10. 11( )5 = 55

11. 18( )3 = 6

12. 5( )2 = 10

13. 8( )6 = 48

14. 13( )2 = 15

15. 16( )5 = 11

Mix-Freeze-Group 107

NORTH, EAST, SOUTH, WEST

1. Arkansas is ___ of Louisiana.

2. Oregon is ___ of Idaho.

3. Oklahoma is ___ of New Mexico.

4. Vermont is ___ of New Hampshire.

5. South Dakota is ___ of North Dakota.

6. Michigan is ___ of Alabama.

7. Washington is ___ of California.

8. Virginia is ___ of Nevada.

9. Montana is ___ of Colorado.

10. Iowa is ___ of Nebraska.

11. Utah is ___ of Missouri.

12. New Jersey is ___ of Ohio.

13. Kansas is ___ of Texas.

14. South Carolina is ___ of Virginia.

15. Idaho is ___ of Arizona.

DO YOU KNOW ME?

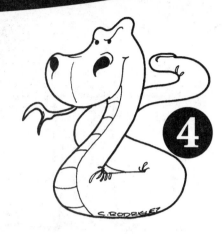

1. I am a cold-blooded reptile.

2. I am an amphibian.

3. I am a warm-blooded mammal.

4. I have feathers and fly.

5. I am an insect.

6. I have gills and live in the sea.

7. I slither on my belly to get around.

8. I nurse my young.

9. I have scales and fins.

10. I used to have a tail, but don't now.

11. I live in a nest.

12. I have wings, but no feathers.

13. I always stay in the water.

14. I say, "Moooo."

15. I live on both water and land.

Mix-Freeze-Group   109

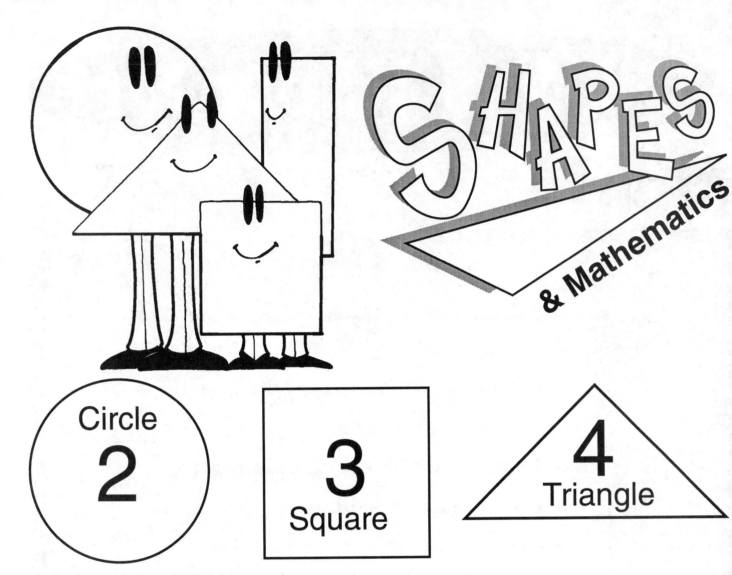

SHAPES

& Mathematics

Circle

2

3

Square

4

Triangle

5

Rectangle

1. I have three sides.
2. I have four equal sides.
3. I have no sides.
4. I have four sides, but not all are equal.
5. Square + Triangle
6. Circle + Square
7. Rectangle - Square
8. Circle + Triangle
9. Rectangle + Circle + Circle
10. Rectangle + Triangle - Circle
11. Circle + Square + Triangle - Rectangle
12. Rectangle + Triangle + Square - Circle

Months

Key

- **January = 2**
- **February = 3**
- **March = 4**
- **April = 5**
- **May = 6**
- **June = 7**
- **July = 8**
- **August = 9**
- **September = 10**
- **October = 11**
- **November = 12**
- **December = 13**

1. I am the last month of the year.

2. I am the fourth month of the year.

3. I am the tenth month of the year.

4. I come after October.

5. I come before June.

6. I am three months before September.

7. I am six months after February.

8. I am nine months before November.

9. Easter is in my month.

10. Christmas is in my month.

11. Halloween is in my month.

12. Thanksgiving is in my month.

13. New Year's Day is in my month.

14. Independence Day is in my month.

15. In leap year, I only have 28 days.

16. I am well known for my showers.

TIME PERIODS

2 **WILD WEST**

MEDIEVAL TIMES **4**

1. People of the time live in caves.

2. People explore other planets.

3. Many people live in the King's castle.

4. Many people live on ranches and farms.

5. In this time, carving are done in caves.

6. Spacecrafts are used to get around.

7. Knights wore armor and carried swords.

8. The skins of animals are used for clothing.

9. To get around, I must walk.

10. Computers are a part of everyday life.

11. People gamble in the saloons.

12. Jousting is a common form of combat.

13. Many people carry around a six shooter.

3 **SPACE AGE**

14. Fire was first discovered and used.

15. To get home, you had to cross the drawbridge over the moat.

5 **STONE AGE**

the 4 Seasons

② Winter   **③** Spring   **④** Summer   **⑤** Fall

1. The leaves begin to fall off the tree.

2. Light showers bring the flowers.

3. The sun is up, and vacation begins.

4. Time to make a snowman.

5. Plants and vegetation is turning green.

6. June, July and August are my months.

7. December, January and February are my months.

8. September, October and November are my months.

9. March, April and May are my months.

10. The snow begins to fall.

11. The animals go into hibernation.

12. Time to go back to school.

13. The days are the longestof the year.

14. The days are the shortest of the year.

Mix-Freeze-Group   113

Mix-N-Match

Students excitedly "Mix" about the classroom as they trade cards; students then look for their perfect "Match," a partner with their matching card.

For Mix-N-Match, students each get a card. With cards in hand, students get up and mill around the classroom trading cards with other students as they pass by. When the teacher calls "freeze," they all stop in their tracks and no more trading of cards is allowed. When the teacher calls, "match" students actively seek out the partner that has their matching card.

Mix-N-Match gets students ac tive with all classmates in a fun way, creating a positive classroom climate.

1 Students "Mix"

After every student gets a card, they get out of their seats and mix through the classroom. As students pass one another "mixing," they switch off cards so that they do not have the same card for very long. "Mix about the classroom. Switch off cards with your classmates as you pass them by. Keep mixing and switching cards until I call, 'Freeze.'"

2 Students "Freeze"

After students mix for a bit, call "Freeze." Students freeze and no longer switch off cards.

4 **Play Again**

After all students have found their perfect match, call "mix" and they start again.

3 **Students "Match"**

When the teacher calls "Match," it is time to find a partner with a matching card. Students mill about the room actively seeking another student with the matching card. When they find each other, they move to the outside of the classroom.

Hints

★ **Open Space.** If possible, play Mix-N-Match in an open space or make some room in the classroom.
★ **Mix Independently.** Encourage students to mix independently, not with friends.
★ **Model.** Model how to find a matching partner.
★ **Move Out.** When students have a partner, they move to the outside of the room to allow more room for those still looking for a partner .

Benefits

• Students enjoy playing, enhancing the class tone. • All students are actively involved looking for their match. • Students interact with many classmates. • Students make connections with partners.

Ideas for My Class!

Classbuilding

- Picture of Students-N-Student Names
- Baby Pictures-N-Students
- Clothing-N-Names
- Furniture-N-Names
- Sports-N-Names
- Movies-N-Actors
- Students-N-Characteristics
- Songs-N-Groups
- Singers-N-Groups
- Celebrities-N-Names
- Pets-N-Names
- Sports-N-Rules
- Artists-N-Artworks
- Cartoons-N-Characters

Mathematics

- Math Problem-N-Solution
- Time-N-Clock
- Digital-N-Analog Time
- Money-N-Value
- Money-N-Equivalent
- Shapes-N-Names
- Angles-N-Degrees
- Numbers -N-Dots
- Mathematicians-N-Accomplishments
- Fractions-N-Equivalents
- Concrete-N-Symbolic
- Mathematics Vocabulary-N-Definitions
- Miles-N-Kilometers
- Pounds-N-Ounces
- Measurements-N-Equivalents
- Dollars-N-Pesos
- Lines-N-Lengths
- Squares-N-Areas

Variations

Snowball Students write a question on a slip of paper and the answer on another slip (or any other matching items). They crumple up the two papers into little snowballs. After every student has two snowballs, half the class gets on one side and the other half gets on the other side and they have a friendly snowball fight. When the teacher calls freeze, students unravel their snowball and try to match up their snowballs.

Principles

Positive Interdependence Every student needs another to make a match.
Individual Accountability Students are responsible for finding their match.
Equal Participation Students participate equally.
Simultaneous Interaction All students mix, freeze and match at the same time.

Science

- Elements-N-Atomic Numbers
- Foods-N-Groups
- Foods-N-Names
- Animals-N-Names
- Transportation-N-Names
- Machines-N-Names
- Laboratory Items-N-Names
- Inventions-N-Inventors
- Inventions-N-Dates
- Scientists-N-Accomplishments
- Bones-N-Names
- Animal-N-Characteristics
- Science Vocabulary-N-Definition
- Organs-N-Names
- Animals-N-Taxonomy

Social Studies

- Countries-N-Names
- States-N-Capitals
- States-N-Names
- Locations-N-Coordinates
- Bodies of Water-N-Names
- Careers-N-Pictures
- Career Descriptions-N-Names
- Countries-N-Flags
- Dates-N-Events
- Rulers-N-Countries
- Governments-N-Countries
- Religions-N-Countries
- Amendments-N-Numbers
- Events-N-Characters
- Presidents-N-Accomplishments
- Types of Architecture-N-Countries
- Vocabulary Words-N-Definitions

Language Arts

- Characters-N-Descriptions
- Vocabulary Words-N-Definitions
- English-N-Foreign Language
- Contractions-N-Words
- Words-N-Parts of Speech
- Sentences-N-Punctuation
- Words-N-Abbreviations
- Authors-N-Books
- Poetry-N-Poets
- Words-N-Synonyms
- Words-N-Antonyms
- Pictures-N-Beginning Sounds
- Capital Letters-N-Small Letters

Mix-N-Match

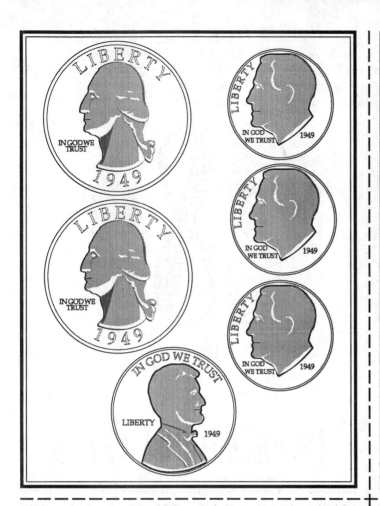

81¢

eighty one cents

36¢

thirty six cents

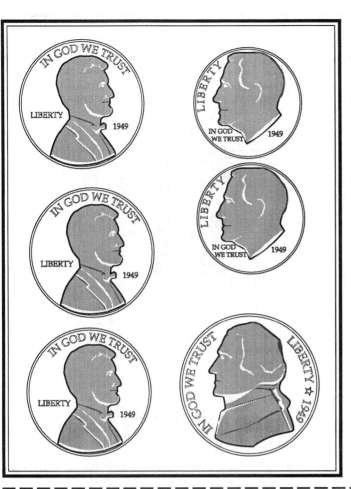

28¢

twenty eight cents

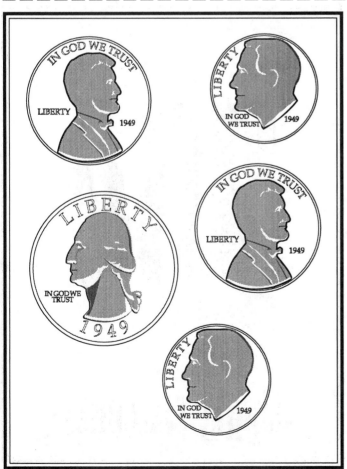

47¢

forty seven cents

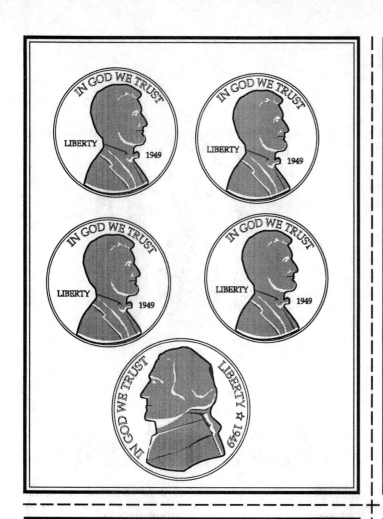

nine cents

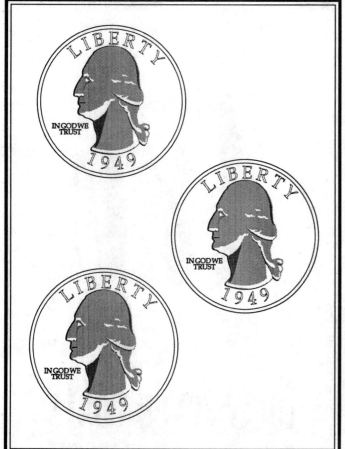

seventy five cents

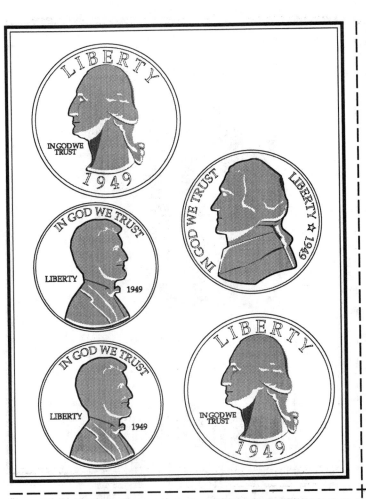

57¢

fifty seven cents

40¢

forty cents

thirty two cents

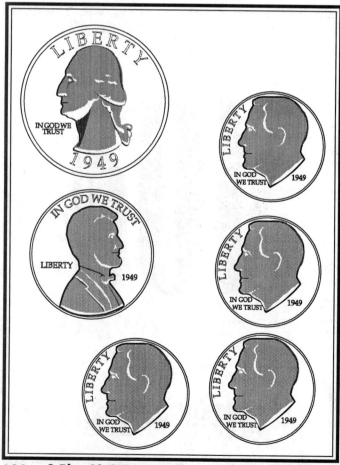

sixty six cents

122 *Mix-N-Match*

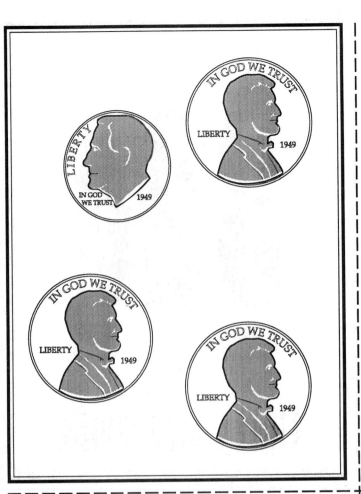

13¢

thirteen cents

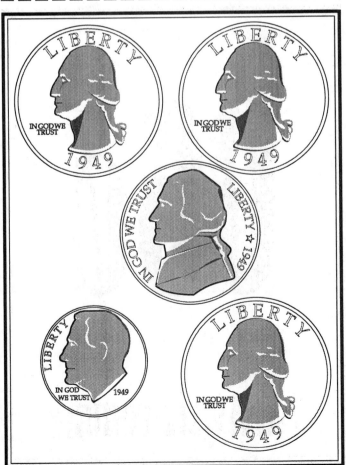

90¢

ninety cents

39¢

thirty nine cents

25¢

twenty five cents

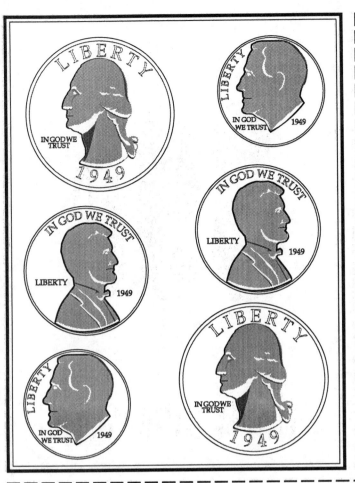

72¢

seventy two cents

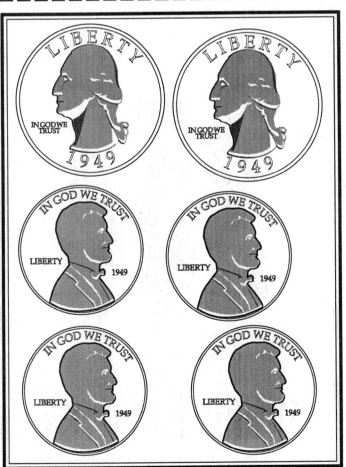

54¢

fifty four cents

Mix-N-Match 125

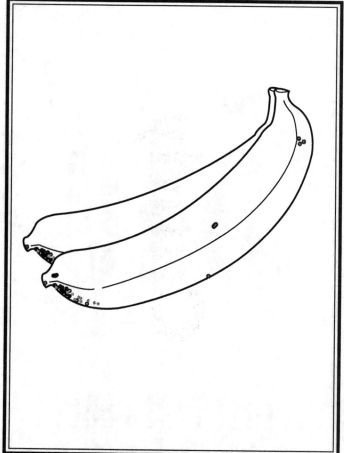

Apple

Bananas

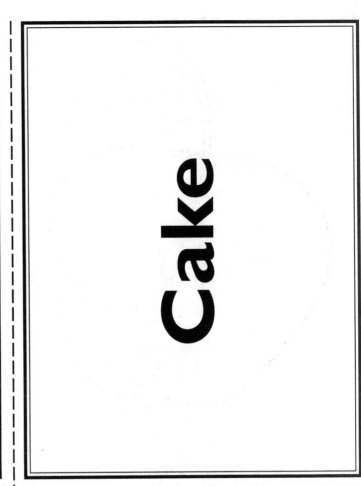

Cake

Candy

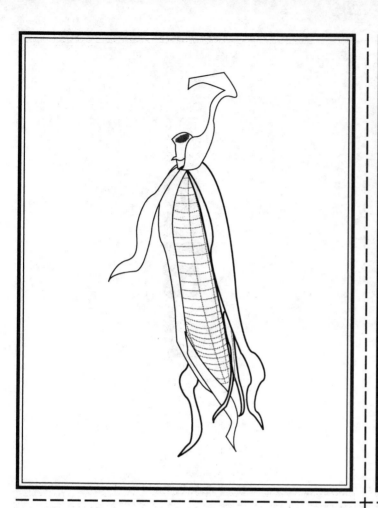

Corn

Doughnuts

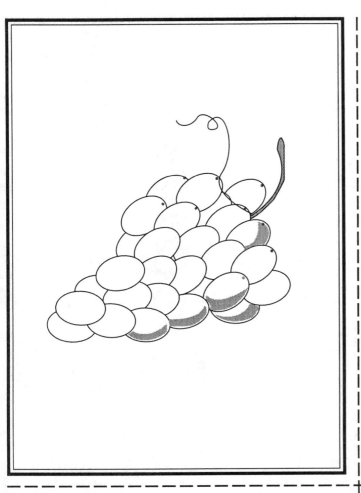

Grapes

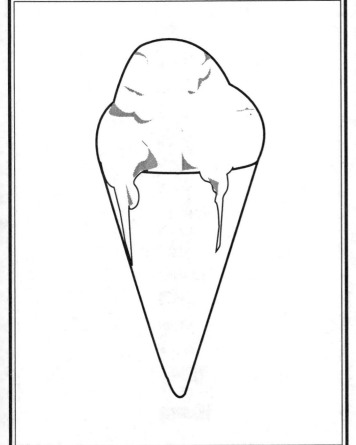

Ice Cream

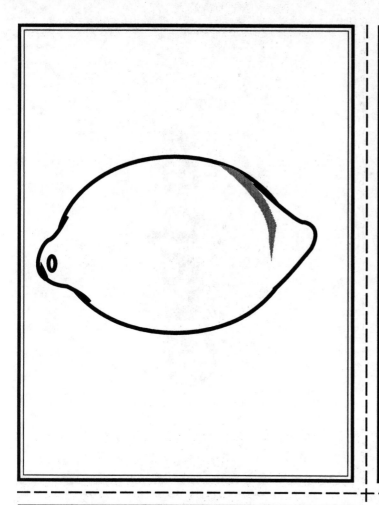

Lemon

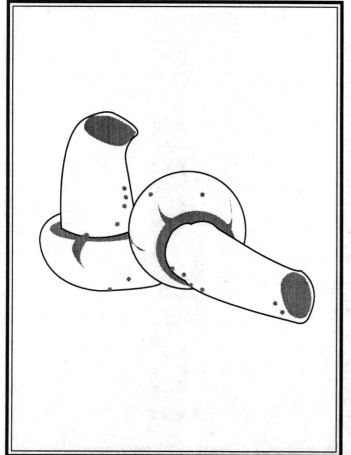

Mushrooms

Pie

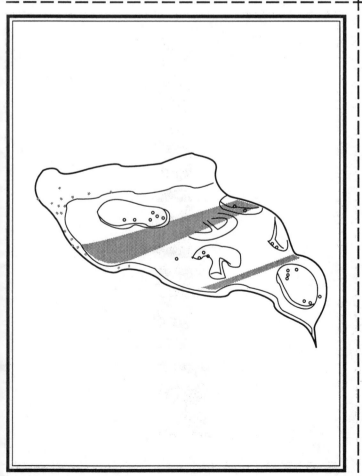

Pizza

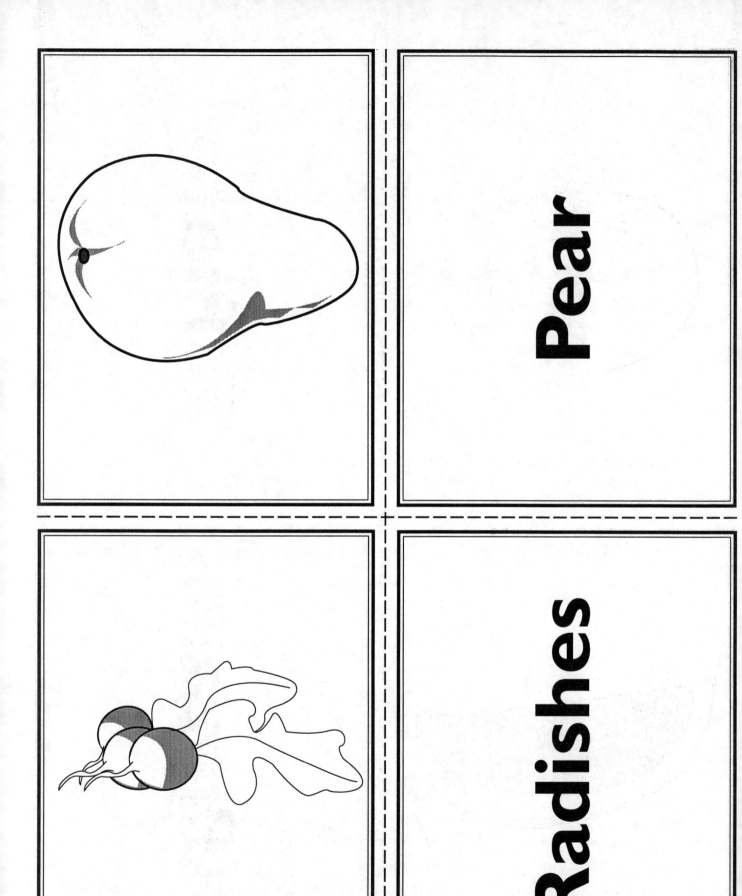

Pear

Radishes

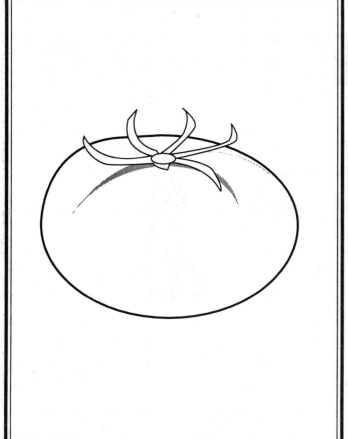

Tomato

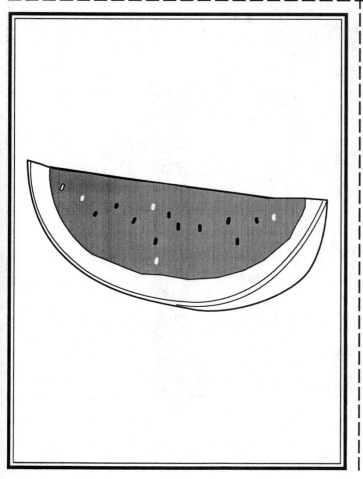

Watermelon

Similarity Groups

Students move about the room forming groups. They discover qualities of their classmates they did not know, and each student makes a special connection with at least one classmate.

The teacher announces a topic and has the students think about the topic. Students then form groups — students with similar characteristics or values group together.

Similarity Groups gets all students actively involved, energizing them while they learn more about their classmates. It is an excellent way for classmates to get acquainted. Students feel mutual support because they discover there are others like themselves. Similarities are the impetus for strong classmate bonds.

1 Teacher Announces Topic

Announce any topic on which students might group. Guide students' thinking by providing imagery about the topic. "Think about your favorite desert. (Long pause.) Think about the last time you had the dessert. (Pause again.) Where were you? How did it taste as you took your first bite? Write down your favorite desert."

2 Students Form Groups

Students get up and move about the class, grouping with those with a similar response. "When I say 'Go,' I want you to get up and form groups. Group with students who like the same or a similar dessert."

③ Pairs Discuss

Have students break into pair discussion within their similarity groups. "Pair up with your closest neighbor, not someone on your team, and discuss what you most like about the dessert."

Ideas for My Class!

Classbuilding

- Favorite subject in school
- Favorite hobby
- Fast food place
- Soft drink
- Pizza toppings
- Color
- Car
- Restaurant
- TV program
- Type of music
- Month born in
- Animal with a tail
- Circus job
- Same number of family members
- Same birth order
- Same numbers in first name

Mathematics

- Geometric shape
- Type of math
- Favorite math manipulative
- Solved the problem same way as you
- Same money value as you (4 quarters, 1 dollar, 2 quarters, 10 nickels)
- Favorite number
- Same answer

Choral Response Have students prepare a "We are..." Choral Response to announce their group. "We are hot apple pie."
Paraphrase Partners After students listen to a partner in their similarity groups, they find a new partner within the group and paraphrase what the old partner said.
Dissimilarity Groups Have students form groups with other students are different from them. This provides the basis for hearing different perspectives.

Principles

Positive Interdependence Students learn to articulate reasons for their preferences as they listen to those similar to themselves.

Individual Accountability Students are accountable to their partner for articulating their reasons.

Equal Participation All students have equal time to share with their partner.

Simultaneous Interaction Students discuss in pairs so that half of the class is discussing at a time.

Science

- Favorite animal
- Favorite insect
- Favorite bird
- Favorite plant
- Favorite dinosaur
- Environment to live in
- Simple machine
- Most important scientific discovery
- Favorite branch of science
- Favorite scientist
- Most common plants in your back yard

Social Studies

- Famous person
- Favorite period of time
- Go back in time
- Favorite state/city
- Continent
- Most important issue facing country
- Famous explorer
- Government job
- Favorite occupation
- Favorite holiday
- Favorite Indian tribe
- American hero
- President
- Wild West character

Language Arts

- Favorite character in the story
- Favorite part of the story
- Favorite type of book to read
- Favorite stage in the writing process
- Favorite author
- Like to write letters to
- Favorite make believe story
- Prediction to the ending of the story
- Sequenced the events in the same order as you

Similarity Groups

Favorite Color

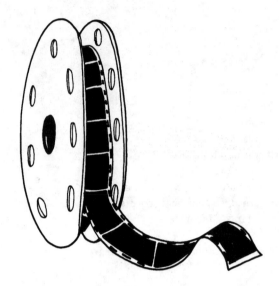

Favorite Movie

_____

Favorite Dessert

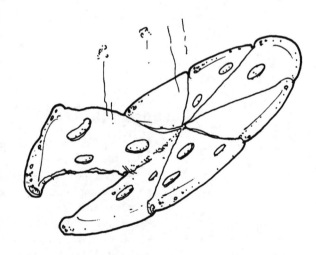

Favorite Food

_____

Name _____

Favorite Book
_____

Favorite Number
_____

Favorite Sport
_____

Favorite Pet
_____

Name _____

Favorite Actor
_____

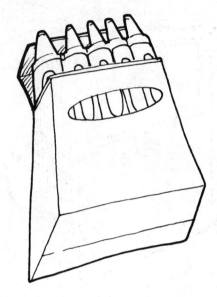

Favorite Artist
_____

Favorite Actress
_____

Favorite Author
_____

Name _____

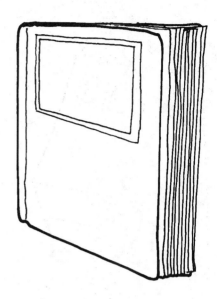

Favorite Subject
_____

Favorite Holiday
_____

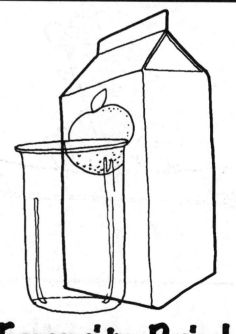

Favorite Drink
_____

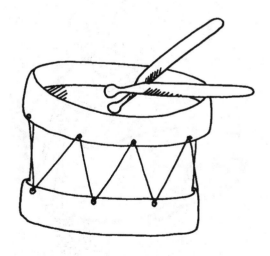

Favorite Band
_____

Name _____

Desert Animal

_____

Jungle Animal

_____

Ocean Animal

_____

Farm Animal

_____

Dinosaur

_____

Bird

_____

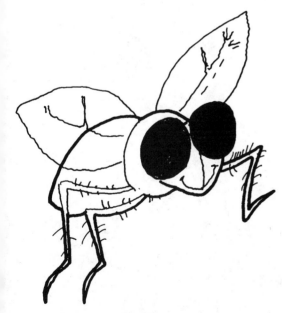

Insect

_____

Reptile

_____

Stir-the-Class

The classroom is transformed into a supportive synergetic think-tank as students move from one huddle to another, sharing ideas, congratulating each other, and building new ideas.

Students stand in groups forming a large circle around the classroom. The teacher presents the class with a problem, and the groups huddle (football style) to discuss the problem. When the groups unhuddle, the teacher "stirs the class" by calling a number to have one student from each group step forward and rotate clockwise to join a new group. Students huddle again to listen to the new member share. After groups congratulate the new member with pats on the back, they unhuddle, standing in a straight line. The teacher provides a new question or discussion topic an d the students huddle again, beginning a new round.

Stir-the-Class is an effective way for students to share information and receive support from a number of different classmates.

1 Students Stand in Groups

Students stand in groups of four. The groups stand in a circle around the classroom. In each group the students stand side-by-side in a line, facing the teacher in the middle of the circle. "We are going to do Stir-the-Class. Each team needs to stand together around the room. Let's form one large circle of teams."

2 Students Huddle

Ask a question or present a problem. Have students turn to face each other with hands on each others' shoulders, as in a football huddle. "What are some possible themes for our class party, and why? Huddle in your groups to discuss. When everyone has something to share, unhuddle and form a line so I know you are ready to share."

4 Huddle Again & Praise

Have students huddle again with their new group and share their ideas. Have students show appreciation for their new member. "Huddle again with your new group. Find out from your newest member what ideas were shared in the last huddle. If you like the ideas you can each give him or her a pat on the back to show appreciation. After that, unhuddle and wait for a new question to discuss."

3 Students Rotate

When the groups all unhuddle, call a number, and ask the students with that number to take a step forward. Then have those students rotate to a new group. "All 'threes,' take a step forward, make a right face, and rotate three ahead to join a new group."

Hints

★ **Model.** Model with some students what a huddle looks like.
★ **Structured Rotation.** Call on ones to rotate one ahead and twos two ahead and so on. That way students don't "meet up" with previous groupmates.
★ **Line Sponge.** Use a Sponge: Tell students that if they finish early while they stand in line, try to come up with additional ideas.
★ **Random Teams.** If you rotate Person 1 one ahead and Person 2 two ahead, and Person 3 three ahead, you will have formed random teams which can sit down together for random team work.
★ **Repeat Topics.** Sometimes do a number of rotations on the same discussion topic to maximize synergy.

Benefits

• Students interact in many groups, with different classmates each time. • Students enjoy the movement, active participation, huddles, and peer support. • Classmates share a variety of ideas from a variety of sources. • Every student is appreciated for his/her contribution. • Teachers get a strong visual clue indicating when groups are ready to share.

Ideas for My Class!

Classbuilding

- Name 3 ways to make this class better
- Two favorite recess activities
- Two favorite TV programs
- Theme class party, food want, games to play
- Class problem: what can we do to solve it?
- How do you spell? (Teacher's name, School, Principal)
- Who's the mystery person?

Mathematics

- Vocabulary shape cards
- Math problems
- Story problems
- Missing add-ins
- Multiplication tables
- Number recognition
- Telling time
- Identifying polygons

Variations

Sharing with the Class Call on a few teams to share their best ideas with the whole class.
Rotating Pairs Call two numbers and have them rotate as a pair. This variation can be used with limited English proficient students who may be "twinned" with a bilingual student to rotate and share together.

Principles

Positive Interdependence Individuals and groups gain form each other: The better the ideas shared in the huddle, the better are the ideas shared in the next huddle.

Individual Accountability Students are randomly selected to share with another team so all students are accountable for listening and sharing.

Equal Participation All students are actively involved in the discussion. Each student rotates and shares one quarter of the time.

Simultaneous Interaction One quarter of the class is speaking at once in the huddle.

Science

- Name five favorite farm animals
- Discuss environmental issues
- Solve simple machine questions
- Properties of magnets
- Properties of electricity
- Dinosaur attributes
- Parts of the water cycle
- Parts of plants & animals

Social Studies

- Where would you find _____ (Peking (in China))
- Vocabulary (What is a water hole in the desert called? (Oasis))
- What is the Capital of? (California (Sacramento))
- Continents
- Which President
- How many?
- Who?
- When? Sequence events
- Identify elements of culture
- Discuss critical issues
- Express opinions on current events
- Identify geographical vocabulary
- Map problem solving

Language Arts

- Vocabulary words (habit-something you do without thinking about it)
- Letter cards: what comes before/after
- Riddle
- Name the tune
- Story character role play
- Vocabulary definitions
- Spelling words
- Identify parts of speech
- Reading comprehension
- New story ending
- Topic sentence of paragraph
- Parts of a letter

Stir-the-Class

You are in the grocery store and you buy five candy bars for you and your friends. Your friends each gave you the money for their candy bar. The cashier only charges you for one candy bar. Do you tell the cashier? If not, do you give your friends their money?

You are walking alone by the school and you notice three kids from another class painting graffiti on your classroom door and window. The next day in school your teacher says there is a $10 reward for anyone who knows anything about the incident. What do you do? Why?

You are playing with a ball at recess and accidentally kick the ball over the fence, and cannot get it back. The next day in class, your teacher notices the ball is missing and starts to blame the student she saw playing with the ball last? What do you do? Why?

Your best friend can get into the school computer to change grades. You are getting a D in history and will be restricted for a month unless you get at least a C. Your friend offers to change your grade. What do you do? Why?

You are walking to the library and see a bully picking a fight with a student in your class. The bully is much bigger than you. What do you do? Why?

You are in a department store and you see a woman take perfume off the shelf and put it in her purse. She is heading for the exit. What do you do? Why?

You are working in teams of four on a project. One student doesn't do hardly any work at all and you and your teammates work really hard. The teacher gives the one student an A and everyone else a B. What do you do? Why?

You get your vocabulary test back and get a perfect 100% score. You are happy and tell everyone at recess and your parents that night. The next day the class goes over the test and you notice that the teacher should have marked three of your answers wrong. What do you do? Why?

Think About It!

Stir-the-Class 149

You are taking an important test and you don't know any of the answers. Your smart friend sitting next to you puts up his paper so you can see his answers. What do you do? Why?

You are a doctor. A child, a teenager, and an adult are all brought into your office. They are all dying and you have no time to ask questions. Who do you help first? Why?

You are doing an art project in the corner of the room with some classmates. You accidentally spill your red paint on the beige carpet. It leaves a huge stain but no one sees you do it. Would you tell the teacher? Why or why or not?

Your brother borrows your friend's bicycle without asking and gets a flat tire. Your brother returns the bike. Your best friend knows nothing about your brother borrowing the bike and asks you if you know anything about the flat tire. What do you say? Why?

You are selected to be one of the two team captains for the kickball game. You have first choice. You can either pick the best player in the class, that doesn't get along with anyone, or you can pick a good player that everyone likes. Who do you pick? Why?

You are in the park playing with some kids you never met before. One of the girls has a bunch of really cool toys you would love to have. Everyone is leaving and almost out of sight. You notice that the girl left one of her cool toys that you really want. What do you do? Why?

You are walking through the grocery store and find two $20 dollar bills on the ground. What would you do? Why?

You come in early from recess and you see a friend going through your teacher's desk. He doesn't see you. The next day in class, your teacher tells to the class that a few of her personal items are missing and would appreciate it if anyone had any information about her stuff. What would you do? Why?

Think About It!

Stir-the-Class 151

Who-Am-I

Students wondering who they are mingle about the classroom questioning classmates, attempting to uncover their hidden identity.

Students each have a picture or a word placed on their backs. They try to find out who they are. To do this, they find a partner. Partners look at each other's backs. They take turns asking each other three questions. The questions are answered only with a "Yes" or "No." After both partners have asked and answered three questions, they mill about the room until they find new partners. They continue until they can guess who they are. When students guess who they are, their partners move their pictures from their backs to their fronts and congratulate them. Those who have discovered their secret identity become helpers. Helpers find a student who still hasn't guessed who they are and drop a subtle hint.

Who-Am-I is a very strong structure to get students actively involved and interacting with their classmates. This structure fosters a positive class tone because students are having fun while interacting with many classmates. Students enjoy helping and being helped.

1 Cards Placed on Backs

Pictures or names are placed on students' backs. A bit of tape will do. If large laminated pictures are used, a hole punch and yarn may be used to create a picture necklace. Care is taken to make sure students don't see their own picture.

2 Students Mix & Pair

Students walk around the room until they find a partner. Partners check each other's back. "Walk around the room until you find a partner. After you shake hands, look at each others' pictures. Then, take turns, each asking three yes/no questions."

5 Students Become Helpers

When students guess who they are, their partner takes the picture off their back and gives it to them to place on their front. Now they are "helpers" and are allowed to drop one subtle hint to any student who does not yet know their identity. A helper might tell Tony: "You're always getting into trouble."

4 Reverse Roles

After Student 1 has asked three yes/no questions, Student 2 asks three yes/no questions.

Continue playing: Students mix and pair up with a new partner, continuing the process until they guess who they are.

3 Student Questions Partner

Student 1 asks his/her partner three yes/no questions trying to find out who is on his/her back. Tony, who has Bart Simpson on his back, asks his partner: "1) Am I a woman? 2) Am I a person? 3) Am I a TV character?"

Hints

★ **Student Content.** Have students come up with the Who-Am-I items (magazines are a good source).
★ **Labels, Name Tags.** Use the self-stick labels from a computer or the type used for name tags.
★ **Laminated Pictures.** Punch two holes out of a piece of paper and tie yarn through the holes to hang the pictures on students' backs. Pictures will be reusable and easy to switch from the back to the front. You can laminate pictures for reuse. Tape works fine too.
★ **No Peeking.** To place pictures on backs, have students form pairs. All Student A's turn their back to the front of the class while Student B's get pictures from the teacher and tape them on Student A's back. Then B's turn their backs while A's get and place pictures.
★ **Hints.** Make sure that helpers don't give away who the other person is. Work on "subtle" hints. Allow them one hint per person so they continue circulating.

Benefits

• Students are actively involved. • Students enjoy the guessing game — and knowing a secret their classmates don't yet know.
• Students learn they need help form others. • Students learn questioning strategies and enhance deductive thinking skills.

Ideas for My Class!

Classbuilding

- Other students in the class
- Teachers in the school
- TV programs
- Cartoons
- Items in the room
- Movies
- Movie Stars
- Pets
- Restaurants in town
- Desserts
- Sports
- Famous athletes

Mathematics

- Number 1-50
- Geometric shape
- Amount of money
- Fractions
- Tools in math (Ruler, Compass)
- Points on a graph
- Mathematicians
- Decimals
- Operations

Variations

Who-Are-We Students can play Who-Am-I in pairs or in teams. Students travel in pairs or in teams to find out who they are. They take turns asking the questions. This variation makes the game easier because fewer pictures are used. To make sure partners or teammates don't see their own picture, students put their arms around each other's shoulders.

What-Am-I Inanimate objects may be used.

Where-Am-I Places may be used.

Identity Storehouse When a student discovers who she is, instead of becoming a helper she can visit the identity storehouse and have a new identity placed on her back.

154

Positive Interdependence Students can't solve the problem without the help of classmates.

Individual Accountability Students are accountable for carefully listening to their partner because they are required to answer. Students are individually responsible for determining their identity.

Equal Participation All students ask and answer questions.

Simultaneous Interaction All students are actively involved in finding out who they are. Students ask questions in pairs.

Science

- Parts of the solar system
- Plants
- Animals
- Famous scientist
- Sea life
- Endangered species
- Things in a rain forest
- Chemical element
- Parts of a cell
- Parts of the water cycle
- Tree leaf
- Dinosaur
- Scientific equipment

Social Studies

- Presidents
- States
- Countries
- Places in town (Bank, Library, School)
- People in community (Nurse, Policeman, Teacher, Fireman)
- Famous people
- Indian tribe
- Culture
- Historical event
- Holiday

Language Arts

- Characters in a book
- Nouns
- Spelling words
- Parts of speech (Verb, Adverb, Adjective)
- Fairy tales
- Punctuation marks (. ! ? ,)
- Nursery rhymes
- ABC's
- Books
- Authors

Who-Am-I

More Who-Am-I Ideas

Things Around School

- Pencil
- Pen
- Crayons
- Calculator
- Desk
- Chair
- Paper
- Book
- Eraser
- Chalk
- Chalkboard
- Projector
- Computer
- Cabinets
- Restroom
- Office
- Classroom
- Library
- Cafeteria
- Auditorium
- Clock
- Window
- Flag
- School Bus
- Bike Rack
- Field
- Basketball Court
- Jungle Gym
- Backboard
- Track
- Playground
- Drinking Fountain

Holidays

- New Year's Day
- Martin Luther King Jr. Day
- Lincoln's Birthday
- St. Valentine Day
- Washington's Birthday
- St. Patrick's Day
- Arbor Day
- Easter
- Summer Vacation
- Mother's Day
- Flag Day
- Father's Day
- Independence Day
- Halloween
- Thanksgiving
- Chanukah (Hanukah)
- Christmas

Fairy Tales & Nursery Rhymes

- Goldilocks
- Hansel & Gretel
- Sleeping Beauuty
- Dumbo
- Peter Pan
- Humpty Dumpty
- Three Little Pigs
- Little Red Hen
- Jack & the Beanstalk
- Snow White
- Puss-in-Boots
- Elves & the Shoemaker
- Little Jack Horner
- Mother Hubbard
- Three Blind Mice
- Three Little Kittens
- Rapunzel
- Beauty & the Beast
- Jack & Jill
- Little Miss Muffett
- Mother Goose
- Frog & Toad
- Pinocchio
- Rumplestilskin
- Cinderella
- Alladin
- Little Mermaid
- Billy Goats Gruff
- Little Red Riding Hood

People in the Community

- Doctor
- Dentist
- Lawyer
- Police
- Fireperson
- Mailperson
- Teacher
- Baker
- Butcher
- Grocer
- Clerk
- Salesperson
- Truck Driver
- Bus Driver
- Delivery
- Printer
- Astonaut
- Businessman
- Stewardess

- Athlete
- Actor
- Musician
- Electrician
- Plumber
- Gardener
- Construction Worker
- Architect
- House Cleaner
- Secretary
- Tailor
- Shoemaker
- Interior Designer
- Operator
- Waiter
- Waitress
- Chef
- Farmer
- Pilot

Who-Am-I 157

Who-Am-I Character Cards

Papa Bear

Mama Bear

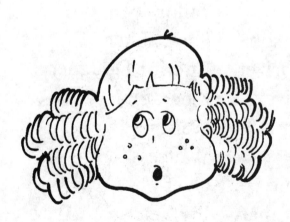

Goldilocks

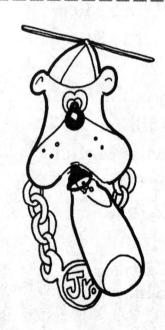

Baby Bear

Who-Am-I Character Cards

Hansel & Gretel

Jack & Jill

Humpty Dumpty

Pinocchio

Who-Am-I Character Cards

Little Red Riding Hood

Sleeping Beauty

Cinderella

Snow White

Who-Am-I Character Cards

Three Little Pigs

Big Bad Wolf

Jack & Beanstalk

Wicked Witch

Where-Am-I State Cards

Alabama

Arkansas

Connecticut

Alaska

California

Delaware

Arizona

Colorado

Florida

Where-Am-I State Cards

Georgia

Illinois

Kansas

Hawaii

Indiana

Kentucky

Idaho

Iowa

Louisiana

Where-Am-I State Cards

Maine   Michigan   Missouri

Maryland   Minnesota   Montana

Massacusetts   Mississippi   Nebraska

Where-Am-I State Cards

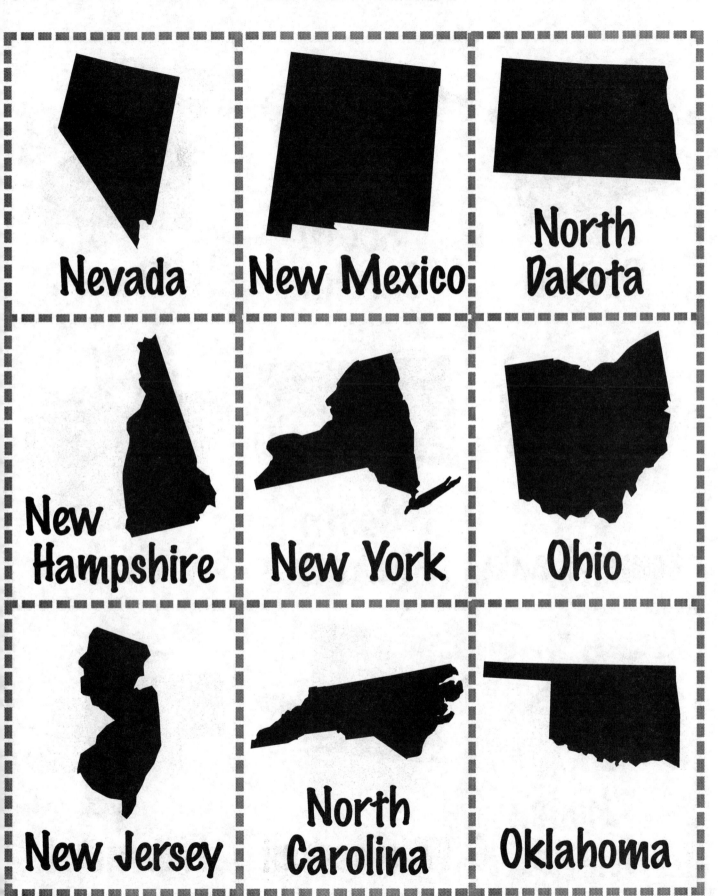

Nevada

New Mexico

North Dakota

New Hampshire

New York

Ohio

New Jersey

North Carolina

Oklahoma

Where-Am-I State Cards

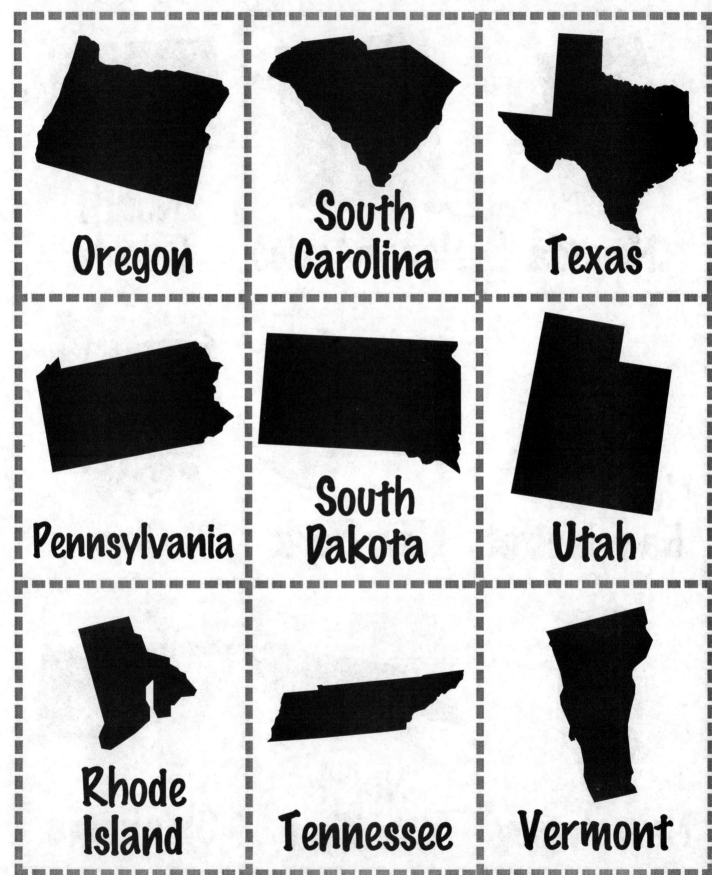

Oregon

South Carolina

Texas

Pennsylvania

South Dakota

Utah

Rhode Island

Tennessee

Vermont

Where-Am-I State Cards

Virginia

Wisconsin

Florida

Washington

Wyoming

California

West Virginia

Alaska

Texas

Resource List

■ Cooperative Learning

Books that promote Classbuilding through the use of cooperative learning

Cohen, Elizabeth G. *Designing Groupwork: Strategies for the Heterogeneous Classroom.* New York, NY: Teachers College Press, 1994.

Gibbs, Jeanne. *Tribes.* Santa Rosa, CA: Center Source Publications, 1987.

Johnson D.W. et al. *Circles of Learning: Cooperation in the Classroom.* Edina, MN: Interaction Book Company, 1993.

Kagan, Spencer. *Cooperative Learning.* San Juan Capistrano, CA: Kagan Cooperative Learning, 1994.

McCabe, M.E. & Rhoades, J. *The Nurturing Classroom.* Sacramento, CA: ITA Publications, 1990.

Shaw, Vanston. *Communitybuilding in the Classroom.* San Juan Capistrano, CA: Kagan Cooperative Learning, 1994.

Kreidler, William J. *Elementary Perspectives: Teaching Concepts of Peace & Conflict.* Cambridge, MA: Educators for Social Responsibility, 1990.

Kreidler, William J. *Conflict Resolution in the Middle School.* Cambridge, MA: Educators for Social Responsibility, 1994.

Levin, Diane E. *Teaching Young Children in Violent Times: Building a Peaceable Classroom.* Cambridge, MA: Educators for Social Responsibility, 1994

■ Social Skills

Books that promote Classbuilding through the teaching of social skills

Bellanca, James. *Building a Caring, Cooperative Classroom.* Palatine, IL: Skylight Publishing, 1991.

Cartledge, G & Milburn, J.F., Eds. *Teaching Social Skills to Children.* Elmsford, NY: Pergamon Press, 1986.

Cowan, D. et al. *Teaching the Skills of Conflict Resolution.* Spring Valley, CA: Innerchoice Publishing, 1992.

Drew, Naomi. *Learning the Skills of Peacemaking.* Rolling Hills Estates, CA: Jalmar Press, 1987.

Feshbach, N. et al. *Learning To Care.* Glenview, IL: Scott Foresman & Company, 1983.

Goldstein, Arnold P. *The Prepare Curriculum: Teaching Prosocial Competencies.* Champaign, IL: Research Press, 1988.

Johnson, D. & Johnson, R. *Teaching Children To Be Peacemakers.* Edina, MN: Interaction Book Company, 1991.

■ The Inclusive Classroom

Books that promote Classbuilding by creating an inclusive classroom

Borba, Michele. *Esteem Builders.* Rolling Hills Estates, CA: Jalmar Press, 1989.

Canfield, J. & Wells, H.C. *100 Ways to Enhance Self-Concept in the Classroom.* Needham Heights, MA: Allyn & Bacon, 1994.

Duvall, Lynn. *Respecting Our Differences: A Guide to Getting Along in a Changing World.* Minneapolis, MN: Free Spirit Press, 1994.

Fox, C.L. & Weaver, F.L. *Unlocking Doors to Self-Esteem.* Rolling Hills Estates, CA: Jalmar Press, 1990.

Grevious, Saundrah Clark. *Multicultural Activities for Primary Children.* West Nyak, NY: The Center for Applied Research in Education, 1993.

Moorman, C. & Dishon, D. *Our Classroom: We Can Learn Together.* Portage, MI: Personal Power Press, 1983.

More terrific ...

Cooperative Learning Resources

Best-Selling Books

- Advanced Cooperative Learning
- Classbuilding
- Communitybuilding
- Cooperative Learning
- Coop. Learn. & Hands-On Science
- Coop. Learn. & Higher Level Thinking
- Coop. Learn. & Integrated Curriculum
- Coop. Learn. & Language Arts
- Coop. Learn. & Mathematics
- Coop. Learn. & Social Studies
- Coop. Learn. & Wee Science
- Coop. Learn. Reading Activities
- Coop. Learn. Writing Activities
- Fraction Fun through Coop. Learn.
- Less. Little Ones: Lang. Arts
- Less. Little Ones: Math
- Resources in Cooperative Learning
- Same-Different
- Science Buddies
- Second Language Learning
- Write! Coop. Learn. & the Writing Process

Hands-On Manipulatives

- Base 10 Manipulatives
- Coop. Learn. ReadingBoards (Various)
- Fold-N-Flash Flashcards (Various)
- Fraction Manipulatives
- Fraction Spinners
- Fraction Fun Combo Kit
- Higher Level Thinking Combo
- Higher Level Thinking Question Cards (Various)
- Idea Spinner
- Match Mine Games (Various)
- Numbered Heads Spinner
- Pop-Up Social Role Card Kit
- Question Manipulatives
- Question Spinners
- Same Different Games (Various)
- Spin-N-Review
- Spin-N-Think
- Student Selector Spinner
- Teamformation Pocket Chart
- Team Selector Spinner

Posters

- 4s Brainstorming
- 28 Multiplication Facts
- Class Rules
- Class Therm. (Great Work)
- Conflict Resolution
- Formations
- Inside-Outside Circle
- Line-Ups
- Numbered Heads
- Pairs Check
- Q-Matrix
- Quiet Signal
- RoundRobin
- RoundTable
- Social Roles
- Terrific Teams
- Think-Pair-Share
- Think-Pair-Square
- Three-Step Interview

Binders

- Coop. Learn. Instructor's Manual
- Coop. Learn. Structures Binder
- Co-op across the Curr. Binder
- Co-op Blackline Binder
- Co-op Facilitators' Handbook
- Co-op Lesson Designs Binder

Videos

- Co-op Co-op
- Fairy Tale Express
- Foundations of CL
- Go Co-op (Down Under)
- Just a Sample
- Numbered Heads Together
- Pairs Check
- Pairs Check & Fractions
- We Can Talk

To order or for a free catalog, call

Kagan

COOPERATIVE LEARNING

1 800 WEE CO-OP
933-2667